The Cuckoo of Instant Presence

THE CUCKOO of INSTANT PRESENCE

The Six Vajra Verses

An Oral Commentary by
CHÖGYAL NAMKHAI NORBU

An Extract from a Retreat at

Merigar, a center of the International Dzogchen Community
in Arcidosso, Italy

December 23, 1985, to January 5, 1986

SHANG SHUNG PUBLICATIONS

First Edition, ed. Cheh-Ngee Goh, Rinchen Editions Pte Ltd, Singapore 1990

Second Edition, ed. Nancy Simmons, Shang Shung Publications, Arcidosso 2018

The glossary of Tibetan, Sanskrit and Oddiyana language terms: Margherita Pansa

© 2018 Shang Shung FoundationPublished by Shang Shung Publications,
an imprint of the Shang Shung Foundation
Merigar
58031 Arcidosso (GR)
http://shop.shangshungfoundation.com

IPC – 1008EN18 – Approved by the International Publication Committee of the Dzogchen Community founded by Chögyal Namkhai Norbu

ISBN: 978-88-7834-164-7

CONTENTS

Editor's Foreword to the First Edition	7
The Six Vajra Verses	9

CHAPTER ONE
General Introduction	11
1.1 The Importance of the Text	11
1.2 History of the Six Vajra Verses	13
1.3 The Significance of the Title	14

CHAPTER TWO
Introduction to Dzogchen	17

CHAPTER THREE
Short Commentary on the Rigpai Khujug	27
3.1 First and Second Verses	29
3.2 Third and Fourth Verses	34
3.3 Fifth and Sixth Verses	36

CHAPTER FOUR
Long Commentary on the Rigpai Khujug	39
4.1 First and Second Verses	39
4.2 Third and Fourth Verses	53
4.2.1 What does "as it is" mean?	53
4.2.2 Refuge, Guru Yoga, Samaya	64
4.2.3 The Practice	75
4.2.3.1 Yowai Nyam	76
4.2.3.2 The Two Defects of Practice	78

4.2.3.3 Thobpai Nyam	79
4.2.3.4 An Account of Five Experiences cited in Dzogchen Semde	80
4.2.3.4.1 The First Nyam	80
4.2.3.4.2 The Second Nyam	81
4.2.3.4.3 The Third Nyam	81
4.2.3.4.4 The Fourth Nyam	82
4.2.3.4.5 The Fifth Nyam	84
4.2.3.5 The Summary of the Practice	85
4.3 The Fifth and Sixth Verses	87
APPENDIX A Brief Guide to the Methods and Traditions of Tibetan Buddhism	99
1 Hinayana and Mahayana: the Path of Renunciation	100
1.1 The Four Noble Truths	101
1.2 The Hinayana	102
1.3 The Mahayana	103
2 Tantra: the Path of Transformation	106
2.1 The Source and Transmission of Tantra	107
2.2 Divisions of Tantra	110
2.3 Higher Tantra	112
2.4 Divisions of Higher Tantra	116
3 Dzogchen, the Path of Self-Liberation	119
ABOUT THE AUTHOR	125
GLOSSARY of Tibetan Terms	127
GLOSSARY of Sanskrit and Oddiyana Language Terms	135

EDITOR'S FOREWORD
to the First Edition

Dzogchen, or Atiyoga, is regarded as the culmination of Buddhist philosophy and meditation practice. For over forty years Chögyal Namkhai Norbu, one of the greatest living masters of this ancient spiritual teaching, has transmitted the knowledge of Dzogchen to an expanding world audience. This book is based on a teaching retreat on *The Six Vajra Verses*, an original Dzogchen text also known as *Rigpai Khujug: The Cuckoo of Instant Presence*, held at Merigar in Arcidosso, Italy, from December 23, 1985, to January 5, 1986, the first complete oral commentary he had given on this important text in the West. Merigar, established in 1981, is the first center of the International Dzogchen Community, a cultural association inspired by Chögyal Namkhai Norbu.

The Six Vajra Verses is divided into three equal parts of two verses each, each explaining the base, the path, and the fruit of the Dzogchen teaching. Ultimately it becomes clear that all three are facets of the primordial state, our real condition as it is and always has been. The *Rigpai Khujug* teaching is presented here first in a concise explanation followed by a detailed one. An appendix titled *A Brief Guide to the Methods and Traditions of Tibetan Buddhism* follows, a teaching given by Rinpoche during a weekend retreat in London in the late 1980s. My hope is that the Dzogchen teaching can thus be more clearly understood in the context of other Buddhist traditions.

Readers less familiar with Tibetan Buddhism who may find the frequent usage of Tibetan terms problematic should understand that the reason Chögyal Namkhai Norbu often employs the original Tibetan nomenclature in his oral teachings is because many Tibetan words have no equivalent in Western languages. Rinpoche encourages his students to avoid misinterpretations and to try to fully understand the meaning of the Tibetan terms. In many cases, an approximate Western term is given after the Tibetan phrase. A glossary is provided at the close of the text. Tibetan words are followed by the Wylie transliteration.

Profound thanks go to many individuals of the Dzogchen Community in the United Kingdom and Singapore for their sustained support in the realization of this book and in particular to the translators of the retreat transcript from Italian to English, Desmond Barry, Andrew Lukianowicz, and John Shane, and to the translator from the Tibetan of the *Rigpai Khujug* verses, John Reynolds.

May all beings benefit from this book.
Bristol, U.K. Cheh Ngee Goh
December 1989

THE SIX VAJRA VERSES

སྣ་ཚོགས་རང་བཞིན་མི་གཉིས་ཀྱང་།
ཆ་ཤས་ཉིད་དུ་སྤྲོས་དང་བྲལ།
ཇི་བཞིན་པ་ཞེས་མི་རྟོག་ཀྱང་།
རྣམ་པར་སྣང་མཛད་ཀུན་ཏུ་བཟང་།
ཟིན་པས་རྩོལ་བའི་ནད་སྤངས་ཏེ།
ལྷུན་གྱིས་གནས་པས་བཞག་པ་ཡིན།

Even though the nature of diversity is nondual,
In terms of individual things, it is free of conceptual elaborations.
Even though there is no thought of what is called "just as it is,"
These various created appearances are ultimately good.
Since everything is complete in itself, abandoning the illness of effort,
One remains effortlessly present in the state of contemplation.

Translated by John Reynolds

CHAPTER ONE
General Introduction

1.1 THE IMPORTANCE OF THE TEXT

The *Rigpai Khujug*, or the *Six Vajra Verses*, is a synthesis of the entire Dzogchen teaching. These verses contain few words and are accompanied by instructions for a practice. Some of the original teachings that Garab Dorje taught and transmitted offer a summary of various Dzogchen tantras called *lung*. Of these several are an abbreviated version of the entire teaching among which one of these principal *lungs* is the *Six Vajra Verses*.

Why are these six one-line verses called the *Six Vajras*? The Vajra symbolizes our own condition, what we call the primordial state. The *Song of the Vajra*, for example, is a song that explains and transmits knowledge of the primordial state. Similarly, the *Six Vajra Verses* can be understood as a synthesis that explains this primordial state. These verses represent the totality of the Dzogchen teaching and a way of understanding it through practice and through developing your knowledge.

However, the significance of the *Six Vajras* will escape you if you see them as merely arid words on a page. The way to understand is through practice, developing knowledge in yourself, whereby the words become the key to understanding and applying the teaching.

Naturally, not only the *Six Vajra Verses* but many of these original texts are like this. Sometimes people with an interest in the teaching learn a certain way of doing a practice given by some master and are satisfied to simply follow a technique. As a result, in many recent traditions of teaching, by learning only how to perform the practice a master has taught them, disciples can remain ignorant of the meaning found in the original texts. Certainly to receive a particular method from a master is important – this is called the Upadesha – but you cannot proceed with a method of a master without understanding its base. The base signifies that the teaching that you follow must have its principle. The teaching, unlike psychology where people can choose the method they prefer and apply it as they wish, is connected to knowledge of the primordial state. This understanding is beyond our judgment and cannot be invented by mental reasoning. If we stay at an intellectual level, we cannot find a correspondence with our true nature.

Everything depends on the *tawa*, the view or the way of seeing. Usually we use our eyes to look outwardly at an object and analyze it. In Dzogchen the approach is different. In the *tawa* of Dzogchen we understand the difference between a mirror and a pair of spectacles. When we look into a mirror, it reflects our existence and our condition. If we have good eyeglasses or binoculars, even if we can see far and perceive details, we are still looking outward. This is the principle: knowing the difference between looking out in dualistic fashion and observing ourselves to discover our own condition. In Dzogchen, whether we refer to a way of seeing or practicing, the principle is always to discover ourselves. Those who have this knowledge concretely transmit all the complex methods to us so that our self-discovery becomes possible.

Doing practice leads to a state called realization. The knowledge of realization was transmitted by those who possessed it, such as Garab Dorje or renowned masters like Padmasambhava and Vimalamitra. The transmission has been handed down from the time of Garab Dorje to the present day. Not only the knowledge but also the texts connected to it, like the *Six Vajra Verses*, have been transmitted throughout the ages. Even if you are interested in Dzogchen, you may not have the possibility or capacity to study the sixty or seventy volumes of original Dzogchen texts that exist. It is much easier to understand a brief and precise text like the *Six Vajra Verses* through your practice and your knowledge. For this reason I will give a short explanation.

1.2 History of the Six Vajra Verses

In Tibetan, the *Six Vajra Verses* is called the *Rigpai Khujug*, probably thus named by Vairochana because this title is not its original one. It is said that at the time of Padmasambhava or King Trisong Detsen, that is, in the eighth century when Vairochana went to Oddiyana to meet the master Śrī Simha, he had great difficulty bringing the texts into Tibet and concealed them by writing with goat's milk on a piece of white cotton. The *Six Vajra Verses* is the first text he introduced.

Not all of the twelve to fifteen volumes of Semde texts are original. Many were added much later, and only few were actually brought to Tibet by Vairochana. The reason is understandable: how could twelve volumes be written on a fragment of cloth with goat's milk? Another text of some thirty to forty pages is also called the *Rigpai Khujug*. This is a Dzogchen tantra and many people think that this is what Vairochana introduced originally, but the truth is that the fundamental part of the *Rigpai Khujug* has only six one-line verses.

Many people say that Dzogchen is not really an authentic teaching, but is an amalgam that includes Chinese Chan. Others who claim that Dzogchen has arisen only recently are ignoring the existence of the large number of very old Dzogchen texts. We need not debate that because the principle of Dzogchen teaching is concerned only with knowledge, not confrontation with the various schools. Nonetheless, something is to be learned from the historical background.

Situated in northeastern Tibet near Amdo at the border with China is Dunhuang, where a vast library existed in ancient times. All the important texts during and after the time of King Trisong Detsen were kept there, eventually remaining for centuries under sand blown down from Xin Jiang and Amdo. Recently this area was rediscovered and Westerners who traveled there brought many of these documents to the West. They can now be found in London and Paris, having become famous as the Dunhuang documents that all scholars consider important and authentic. The *Rigpai Khujug* and its commentary, a text probably written by Vairochana, have also been found among these documents, a clear proof that Dzogchen is an authentic and ancient teaching.

1.3 The Significance of the Title

When Vairochana introduced the Six Vajra Verses in Tibet he called them *Rigpai Khujug: The Cuckoo of Instant Presence*. The full title is *Tashipai Pal Rigpai Khujug*. *Tashipai* is a talisman of good fortune, *pal* means glory, *rigpa* is the state of knowledge, the presence of the pure state of awareness, and *khujug* is the cuckoo. In Tibet the cuckoo is a symbol of nature breathing again. When the cuckoo's song is heard everyone is happy because it is a sign that the long, icy winter is finally going. Spring appears, plants begin to grow, and poor animals like the yaks and horses that found little to eat under the snow are now certain that they will not die. A Tibetan who does not hear the cuckoo's song will search in the mountains to do so. The name *chawön* or deaf to the cuckoo's cry, given a person who has not heard the cuckoo for a long time, is applied to those who have a weak constitution and consequently a condition like low blood pressure. Such a person is urged to hear the song as soon as possible, not that the sound itself is the reinforcing medicine needed, but that it represents a cure related to the arrival of the new season.

The title *Rigpai Khujug* is a message of coming glory using nature to mirror the significance Vairochana gives to the introduction of the Dzogchen teaching for the first time in Tibet. Because of the symbolic meaning of the cuckoo, he cites that bird in the title of this text.

Before Vairochana, the great translator and first Tibetan master of Dzogchen, introduced the *Rigpai Khujug* in Tibet no particular Dzogchen teaching of Atiyoga existed there. Padmasambhava had introduced and given some Dzogchen teaching but always Dzogchen in the context of Anuyoga, linked to its method of transformation. In order to introduce Atiyoga Dzogchen into Tibet, Padmasambhava sent Vairochana to India to meet his master Śri Simha to receive the teaching. The *Rigpai Khujug* is the first Dzogchen text that was translated, transmitted, and introduced in Tibet, making it an extremely important text.

CHAPTER TWO
Introduction to Dzogchen

What is Dzogchen? Truly speaking, Dzogchen is our condition. When we gather in a retreat, I always explain an understanding of our own condition. Even though I describe it in different ways, what we call Dzogchen, Total Perfection, is our own condition. If you understand this, a real basis for your development is present. When a person lacks this knowledge, he or she is said to suffer from *marigpa*, ignorance.

In Dzogchen, ignorance is not what we normally mean by that term. Ignorance generally implies a poor education, but in the Dzogchen sense a well-educated person can also be ignorant, whereas a person with no education is not necessarily ignorant. We do not deny the value of education or imply that it is the base of ignorance. Education used in the right way can be valuable, but more usually it is an obstacle to spiritual development.

Take people who are single-mindedly devoted to Eastern philosophy, for example. Why are they fixed in this way? It is because Western philosophy does not satisfactorily relate to their situation and has not convinced them. As a result, they want to go deeper into something else even though this still involves study and mental analysis. Such people's declaration of agreement with what Buddha or Nagarjuna says is just a mental decision to believe that things make more sense than in Western philosophy or in a certain way of seeing. People like this want to enter Buddhist, Hindu, or Confucian thought, already convinced about what is yet to be studied in those Eastern philosophies. Day by day they develop and deepen this conviction and feel rich in knowledge, but in fact they have conditioned themselves with their ideology. People who are convinced by everything Nagarjuna says in Buddhist philosophy have become perfect slaves to Nagarjuna's ideology. They will automatically disagree with other Buddhist schools or with Hindu philosophy, and while their conviction might seem marvelous, it is false, because any view constructed only through study or ideology can collapse.

In Dzogchen you should not construct anything false. You have to understand the real condition and what you are doing. *Tawa*, the way of seeing, means discovering what really is. Generally *tawa* refers to the way the philosophy of a particular school is explained. For example, in the Mahayana the way of seeing of Nagarjuna is considered perfect. Someone who has learned it tends to criticize the views that disagree with what Nagarjuna taught. Those more inclined toward the Nyingma tradition will try to learn what Longchenpa taught and will use Longchenpa's writings to defend the Nyingmapa view. That is what *tawa*, the way of seeing, normally means.

The way of seeing in Dzogchen, however, is not about looking outside and judging. What is involved in Dzogchen is to find ourselves in the state of knowledge. Again, to use the example of a mirror and eyeglasses, glasses are for looking outward at external objects, an example of dualism. The principle in Dzogchen is the mirror: we look at it to discover ourselves. When you decide to follow a master, you should not blindly believe everything he says. A master is not a commander at whose every word you jump to attention, saying, "Yes sir," nor should you seek out a master simply to argue with him. It is a mistake to enter into conversation with a master just for the sake of discussion because that is another case of mental reasoning. We have been using the intellect since time immemorial and have resolved nothing. We cannot stop the process of transmigration with further reasoning. The point is that you have to try to understand what the master is explaining. The master is not creating another mental construct for you. He is simply trying to give you a method to discover yourself. It is up to you to try to understand and apply the method. Naturally, a master can advise and give methods and practices to help you to arrive at knowledge, but he definitely cannot perform a miracle to change you and give you instant enlightenment.

Some people follow various teachers for years without resolving anything, and then, when they hear of another master, rush to get teachings, hoping that they can now finally be enlightened. No master is capable of that. The power of a master lies in his ability to explain the teachings. When a student has received the method, applied it, and truly entered into the state of knowledge, then we can say the master has really performed a miracle.

Sometimes, however, it is difficult for the master to do this, because a disciple also has to have a certain capacity. For example, when I was in Nepal, many Sherpas came to me to and offer rice, money, and white scarves called *khatags* and to receive blessings, leaving without asking for teaching. I knew that they could benefit from understanding the teachings, but what could I do if they were not interested? People come passively, thinking, "Oh, this master is a great reincarnation, I should create a good cause and a good relationship by offering some rice or money. I will get a blessing and everything will be alright." Certainly one can establish a good cause by making an offering, but a good cause can also be made by a dog or a cat. When a human being who can speak, can reason, and has higher capacity than a dog comes only for a blessing, it is sad. You must not be passive in this way. You must know that what a master teaches is to be understood and applied in practice. There is a famous saying of Buddha Shakyamuni, "I show you the way, but realization depends on you." Even the Buddha, who is fully enlightened with all possible capacities, omniscient and possessing infinite compassion for the suffering of all beings, could not illuminate us. If he could give only the teaching and practice, how can anyone else do better?

Generally the teaching is summed up in three principles: the base, the path, and the fruit. This is characteristic not only of the Dzogchen teaching, but also of Buddhist Sutra and Tantra. In Buddhist Sutra, the base is said to be the understanding of the two truths: absolute truth and relative truth. With this base it is considered that there are two accumulations on the path, one of merit and the other of wisdom. The accumulation of merit is related to the relative truth on the relative level of our body, speech, and mind. For the body, this means doing positive actions such as prostrations; for the voice, reciting mantras, praying, and avoiding negative actions like insulting and provoking people; and for the mind, cultivating compassion and avoiding negative thoughts such as hatred. In this way, we accumulate merit linked to the three aspects of our existence resulting in the elimination of obstacles and helping us onto the path of wisdom. That is also why in Tantric practice in order to overcome obstacles and to purify oneself, one does ngöndro (preliminary practices). One can then enter into the practice of meditation and contemplation, the path of wisdom. In Sutra, the main method is to follow the path of accumulation of good actions and purification before arriving at the path of wisdom. However, although Sutra does not consider the accumulation of merit the more important of the two, it implies that without the accumulation of merit it is not easy for a person to enter the path of wisdom and progress in it. Upon attaining enlightenment, Buddha said, "I have found a path to the state of knowledge that is luminous, profound, and clear, beyond explanation and concept. If I try to explain it, no one will understand." Why would no one understand? Because the experience of the path of wisdom is beyond explanation. In despair the Buddha said, "I will go back to the forest to meditate."

CHAPTER TWO *Introduction to Dzogchen*

A well-known Dzogchen invocation says that to explain this meaning even the Buddha's tongue is weak. It does not mean that the Buddha did not have a perfect way of communication; the sutras list sixty unique qualities of voice that the Buddha possesses. Rather, it implies that the Buddha had no way of explaining this experience because it is beyond the relative level.

The way of application of the absolute truth in Sutra is called the way of wisdom. For example, in Chinese Chan or Japanese Zen Buddhism, the emphasis is less on the accumulation of merit than on understanding the absolute truth and direct entrance on the path of wisdom. That is why there are the so-called gradual path and the nongradual path. We can enter the path of wisdom either gradually by first accumulating merit and doing purification practice or nongradually, by directly entering the path of wisdom.

Both those who follow the gradual and nongradual paths talk about the fruit, the result of the practice. The fruit in both cases is total realization and illumination. In Buddhism, we often refer to the dimensions of enlightenment as *kayas*. *Kaya* means dimension, the condition that is all of existence. It does not mean "body" as is usually understood. We often talk about the two or three bodies, as if separate Buddhas gained enlightenment in differing ways. The fact is that each one of us has the essence of the Buddha, the different *kayas* or dimensions within ourselves, but our ignorance is such that we fail to understand this, making an explanation of the base and the path necessary.

In Sutra, we usually talk about two dimensions or two manifestations, in Sanskrit called the *dharmakaya* and the *rupakaya*. *Dharma* means existence, the knowledge and the understanding of existence, and it is also the path. If something needs to be understood, then there is a way of understanding and that is the path. Buddha enabled people to understand what existence is. We ourselves are existence. This is the knowledge Buddha taught. That is what Dharma refers to, and it is not some kind of limited religion. *Dharmakaya*, therefore, refers to the dimension of the understanding of existence.

Rupa means form, and *rupakaya* refers to the enlightened dimension of form. In Tantrism, *rupakaya* is subdivided into *sambhogakaya* and *nirmanakaya*, because two kinds of form exist, pure and impure. Enlightened beings who manifest through light are said to be a pure vision. Ordinary beings manifest physically as human, dog, cat, ant, and so on as a result of karma and are considered to be an impure vision. *Rupakaya* implies no such distinction; it can be the first or the second kind of vision.

What does it mean when an enlightened being has the form of a human or an animal? Two distinct principles are to be considered here: a being who freely chooses to take a physical form such as that of a human being and a being who takes that form on account of karma. If Buddha manifests as an elephant in order to teach elephants, that elephant would be radically different from a normal elephant. Buddha was not obliged to take that form as a result of past karma: he manifested that way through his own will, whereas other beings take the form of an elephant and that becomes their karmic vision just like the form of any other being would. That Buddha voluntarily assumes this form explains why an enlightened being can appear on the *rupakaya* level of impure vision. In Sutra, because the base is explained in terms of the two truths, we have the two accumulations on the path, and as the fruit the manifestations of *dharmakaya* and *rupakaya*, the two dimensions.

The base, the path, and the fruit exist in Tantrism as well. The principle of Tantric teaching is founded on two forces, the masculine and the feminine, or the lunar and the solar. That is why Tantra is taught and explained through the manifestation of energy. This principle is based on *e* and *vam*, emptiness and manifestation, respectively referred to as *sherab*, wisdom, *thab*, method.

CHAPTER TWO *Introduction to Dzogchen*   23

How does one enter into this understanding and knowledge and how does one develop it? On the path, since the two ways of application are *kyerim*, the development stage, and *dzogrim*, the completion stage, the fruit is explained in the same way as in Sutra, with the two dimensions. In Tantrism the base can be explained by way of the Three Vajras representing the true state of existence of our body, voice, and mind. In terms of the path, the solar and lunar forces are represented by *kyerim*, *dzogrim*, and *sungjug* (the union of the two); consequently the fruit in this case is referred to as the *dharmakaya*, *sambhogakaya*, and *nirmanakaya*, the three dimensions.

Some types of Tantrism are based on our five aggregates. In terms of the path, we use our five passions and transform them so that they manifest as the five wisdoms. Finally, these manifest as the five dimensions of illumination: the usual three with the addition of *ngowo nydiku*, or *svabhavikakaya*, the dimension of the union of the first three dimensions, and *dorjei ku*, or *vajrakaya*, the dimension of the Vajra, representing the state of integration with the manifestation. In Tantrism, then, the base, path, and fruit can be explained in various ways. We can understand from these examples that these three principles are present in Sutra and Tantra as well as in Dzogchen.

Dzogchen is the way of self-liberation. In this case the base is the primordial state of every individual. Those who are more familiar with Sutra speak of the essence of the *tathagata*. Those who have a knowledge of Tantrism refer to the Vajra. For example, *sems dpa' rdo rje*, or *sattvavajra*, is the Vajra of the mind, more generally referred to as nature of mind. In Dzogchen we speak of the primordial state, also represented by many other designations. The word Dzogchen itself refers to the base. *Dzog* means perfected, implying that nothing is missing and everything is included, while *chen*, usually translated as great or large, here means total. Dzogchen signifies that in this primordial state, nothing is lacking, everything is perfect.

Regardless of the term by which Dzogchen is identified, a transmission from a master is needed to open that state of knowledge in the individual, a state that has to be made real, or in other words, realized. Many different types of methods exist for this purpose. The master explains and transmits the knowledge and the methods, collaborating with individuals, helping them to help themselves. It is not that a miracle happens and everything becomes automatically fine.

Many people wonder why you need a master if you want to follow the Dzogchen teachings. Why is it not enough to read a book that explains everything properly? It is not that a book has no value, but it depends much on the person. People who follow Dzogchen have a good and exact causal connection with it, otherwise they certainly would not meet this teaching. If a person does not have that precise cause, but nevertheless has a certain awakened quality, reading a book might be useful. Ideally one should follow a true Dzogchen master because such a teacher has the living transmission that has been handed down from the source of the teaching. He or she can use this transmission to work with the individual at the level of body, voice, and mind, making it much easier for that student to find himself or herself in the state of knowledge and no longer in confusion. In Tibetan we say that the person is then no longer like a little dog that has lost its way in the fog. The master also knows how to develop and to continue the application of knowledge using different methods according to the specific need of an individual. That is why students can make great progress with the aid of a master.

The Dzogchen teaching is a living knowledge that is transmitted and applied. It is not reserved for spiritual adepts. The teaching is useful for those who want to live agreeably. For someone with strong faith, it is extremely useful. Even those who do not believe in anything and think that nothing exists after death could find a more peaceful life through it. To enjoy tranquility, you must have experience of the state

CHAPTER TWO *Introduction to Dzogchen*   25

of knowledge and know how to relax. When you discover your true condition and actually find yourself in it, you finally understand the real meaning of relaxation. Until then, although you might think you are relaxed, your state is still a construction of the mind.

We always use this word "relax." It is easy to say, "Relax, relax. Don't be tense," but most people do not understand how to relax at all. Some people know how to relax the body a little by stretching out on a bed; others may relax bodily energy by doing breathing exercises. These are ways of relaxing at the relative level linked to time, and time is linked to secondary conditions.

Now I am relaxed. Everyone greets me with, "Merry Christmas." They give me sweets or presents. Why should I be nervous? I feel wonderful. Why? Because of circumstances: the secondary causes are positive, but maybe tomorrow it might snow, and we might have no more water with no possibility of going out. Then someone could arrive who instead of bringing a gift, presents me with an argument. Certainly in those circumstances, it is more difficult to relax. Relative conditions are connected to time, so everything changes. Even if you manage to relax your body, speech, and mind, it will always be provisional if tied to relative matters. That is why the teaching is necessary.

Buddha explained that samsara is characterized by suffering. This is real, not just a subject of conversation. Whether we observe ourselves or others, we can see that there is always suffering. Whoever does not know how to relax will become ever more tense when a problem arises. We know that when we are in a hurry we get anxious and nothing gets done. People who wake up late in the morning and then have to rush to the office put their pants on backwards or their sweater inside out. Ready to leave the house they cannot find their keys. Everybody has such experiences upon occasion. They demonstrate that when we are under duress we have problems, and simple things become complicated. You might know intellectually, "I must not get nervous. I must relax," but it is not that easy. You need to apply a particular knowledge, and that needs a base. The Dzogchen teaching is a way of relaxing totally, so you can understand why the learning, application, and practice of Dzogchen is indispensable for every individual.

CHAPTER THREE
Short Commentary on the Rigpai Khujug

The *Rigpai Khujug*, like all Dzogchen teachings, enables us to have a deeper understanding of our own situation. As we approach the teaching, we should not regard it as an external object to be observed. Rather, we have to look into ourselves, because the teaching is for reflecting our own condition.

The three principles in the teaching called *zhi*, *lam*, and *drebu*, the base, the path, and the fruit, apply to all levels of teaching. The first of these three is known as the base. People tend to explain the base as the origin from which all phenomena arise, but it does not matter what term is used. Even if you know many terms, so long as you have not really understood what the base means, you are still far from the meaning of the teaching. The real base is ourselves. How can we begin to approach this understanding and when we have it, how do we develop ourselves? That is what is termed the path. The path is the method by which we can evolve until we arrive at realization, the fruit, a certain state of knowledge that is not just a word or an idea but something real. If you want to know what the path and the fruit are, you must first understand what the base is, otherwise you have no starting point, like a house that must have a foundation or it will collapse. In order to understand our base, we have to observe our own condition.

While Buddhist Sutra uses the terms base, path, and fruit as well, it also posits the famous two truths, relative and absolute truth. In the

Dzogchen teaching, we do not speak so much of the two truths, but if you have an understanding of what they are, you can easily grasp what is meant by the base in Dzogchen.

Speaking of our existence, we refer to the mind and the nature of the mind. It is not necessary to define one as the relative and the other as the absolute. The nature of the mind is the condition of things as they are, but it is not possible to understand this condition if we do not really know our situation. The capacity of a mirror refers to its ability to reflect with clarity, purity, and limpidity. These terms give us an idea: if we did not know what a mirror was, how could we understand clarity, purity, and limpidity? The same is true of our existence of body, speech, and mind. An intellectual understanding is not enough. What we need is real knowledge.

Knowing at an intellectual level is not so difficult. Whether a person has intellectual or real knowledge depends on whether what the person understands corresponds to reality. Take someone who has studied many Buddhist sutras. Such a person would have some understanding of the term *shunyata* or voidness. One of the many ways to understand this concept, for example, is by examining an object. Through a mental process you dissolve the object into its atoms and thus into voidness. Although that object has not really turned into nothingness, if you carry out this intellectual process at a certain point, you arrive at a state called *nangtong* where the mind spontaneously enters into the state of voidness. That is what we mean by an actual experience of what was previously an intellectual understanding. This experience can be followed by an explanation of how the entire material world is an illusion. If what appears has no actual substance, what is there other than illusion? Certainly we understand this intellectually. Even if we know everything is illusory, in practice due to our attachment things seem real to us. When you have a severe headache, you can tell yourself that the headache is illusory. If by only thinking

CHAPTER THREE *Short Commentary on the Rigpai Khujug* 29

in that way you can get rid of the headache, you can say that your knowledge really corresponds to reality. Otherwise your knowledge has remained at the intellectual level. That is why, first of all, we must have a genuine understanding.

Of the three fundamental aspects of the teachings, the base, the path, and the fruit, the path is defined as *tawa*, the way of seeing; *gompa*, the way of practice; and *chöpa*, the attitude, our conduct or behavior, referring to how we integrate our practice with whatever we do. The *Rigpai Khujug* is divided into three sections of two verses each, corresponding to three topics base, path, and fruit.

3.1 First and Second Verses

སྣ་ཚོགས་རང་བཞིན་མི་གཉིས་ཀྱང་།
ཆ་ཤས་ཉིད་དུ་སྤྲོས་དང་བྲལ།

natsog rangzhin minyi kyang
chashe nyidu trö tang tral

Even though the nature of diversity is nondual,
In terms of individual things, it is free of conceptual
    elaborations (made by mind).

Natsog means diversity, referring to the way phenomena manifest at the level of appearance. In our human vision, we see numerous things, each one distinguishable from another. For example, if we see two people, we see two diverse beings. A single person alone is composed of various parts, like the nose, the ears, the eyes, the hair, and so forth. Whatever is distinct or dissimilar in our vision is called *natsog*.

We usually consider three types of vision. The first is called *lenang*, karmic vision. For example, an ordinary person's karmic vision is a result of certain causes produced by the passions. A second type of vision is *nyamnang*, the vision of practitioners on the path. When we relax our body, voice, and mind as well as our elements, we can have *nyams*, experiences arising from practice. Such visions appear not as a result of having purified our karma, but because our energy expands when we relax. The third kind of vision is *dagnang*, pure vision. Karmic vision is impure and arises due to a cause. If this cause is eliminated, we have pure vision. That is why we say that a realized person has pure vision. Whichever visions we have, all are part of *natsog*.

If we analyze phenomena in every single detail, we have a collection of an infinite number of things. Take our karmic vision as an example. The causes of karmic vision are the five or six passions that lead to the five or six *lokas*, or realms. Accumulated as causes, other types of passions, such as the 84,000 mentioned in Sutra, will also produce diverse corresponding effects that manifest as different karmic visions. Many of these visions are unknown to us because as human beings we are familiar only with our own condition. *Natsog* means the many different conditions that can exist.

Rangzhin means nature, the real condition of these infinite aspects that exist; *minyi* means nondual, where *mi* in Tibetan is negative and *nyi* two. The nature of all these millions of aspects is nondual. What does this actually mean? In the Dzogchen teaching, we do not have considerations such as "that is not dual," "there is no difference," or "all nature that exists is one." Let me explain: In considering the two truths, Buddhist Sutra says that everything you see around you is part of the relative truth and its condition is void. This real condition is the absolute truth. When you sit in lotus position with the hands joined and spine straight and are internally relaxed, you can enter into a state of *shunyata* or voidness, and you can be said to be in the absolute truth. When you finish your practice, get up, and start walking around, that condition is the relative truth. This is like having two legs, with one the relative truth and the other the absolute truth. You step ahead with the leg of relative truth, then with the leg of absolute truth, and so on. When we talk about *dennyi sungjug*, the union of the two truths, clearly the two legs are two separate things.

In Dzogchen, nondual does not mean two things united. Nondual means that from the beginning the two truths approach does not apply. We therefore have to discover for ourselves what is the state of nonduality in all these aspects. This is important as a way of seeing phenomena and as a base for understanding. When we do practice, for example, we can have millions of *nyams*. or experiences, but if we find ourselves in the state of contemplation, of Dzogchen in our real condition, we can experience nonduality. We cannot say that one *nyam* is the same as another, nor can we cancel or erase the different aspects of a *nyam*. We do not do something mentally, neither erase nor unite. This is an important point and we must understand it well.

Someone involved in an experience is not at a high level of practice. A person absorbed by the sensation of pleasure is not in contemplation. To be in a state of void where the voidness is really frightening is not contemplation either. Both are called experiences. Many practitioners remain in a state of experience but believe that they are in the state of contemplation. This is called an obstacle.

The aspects of experiences are different. Someone who is experiencing pleasure and remains for days like this smiling in that sensation, believing to be in the state of contemplation, and someone who stays hour after hour in a state of voidness and a little frightened, also convinced that of being in contemplation, both share the *"nyam"* of having fallen asleep in the experience. In the Dzogchen teaching, such experiences are not considered contemplation. The contrast between a person who has a smile on his face and another who is frightened is called *natsog*. If a hundred people have experiences, each slightly different from the others, that is *natsog*.

Rangzhin minyi means not simply remaining in the condition of the experience, but using the experience as a method to find oneself in the state of contemplation. In these experiences we are present and not as if in a swoon or a state of having lost consciousness. There is no difference whatsoever whether this presence is found in the experience of the person who is smiling or in that of the person who is frightened, even though the experiences are completely different. *Minyi* does not mean that two things are united or that we think that they are the same. If we say that the nature of those things is not real and thus they are the same, our judgment remains as a mental construction. But if we go through the diverse experiences and hence find that the true state of presence found in all of them has no difference, then the real state of *natsog* is won, and the presence is called *rigpa*. Though different experiences are not the same, this is what we mean.

Someone who does not have this knowledge follows a teacher to apply the teaching he or she transmits and develop this understanding. Even if we do not possess this knowledge of our nature and the real condition, the base is always there, like a mirror, which has the capacity to reflect whatever is in front of it, the secondary causes. The base means that although diverse things manifest, the inherent nature is one, called the primordial state. *Kyang* means however.

In the second verse *chashe*, translated here as individual things, refers to the individual parts of the diversity of phenomena: *cha* corresponds to a part of something, *she* to something that belongs to a group. *Nyid* means the real state of a single thing, *trö tang tral* means beyond consideration or judgment. What, then, is the real meaning of *chashe*? True knowledge is beyond the consideration of the two truths. With regard to the relative truth, we say everything manifests before us. In the Dzogchen teaching, another way of saying that is *yulden kadag*: *yul* means object, *den* something real that actually appears, and *kadag* pure from the beginning. This is an important point for understanding

CHAPTER THREE *Short Commentary on the Rigpai Khujug*

the Dzogchen teaching. This tent, for example, which appears to all of us as yellow, red, and so forth, is what we can call our common karmic vision because we are human beings. Why are we human beings? Because we have that karma. We see everything equally as a result of the same cause, but that does not mean that our cat sees things in the same way we, do nor will a little bird or an insect. Therefore, vision exists in different ways, and a stable, universal vision does not exist. *Chashe* means belonging to, part of, or characteristic of all the individual things; it is the apparition of the energy of every single individual. The apparition is considered to be pure from the beginning: nothing exists, but everything belongs to or is characteristic of our primordial state. Everything manifests in this way. When we are in that state and have knowledge of our condition as it really is, there is nothing to establish with respect to how things should be. That is why it is called *trö tang tral*, beyond concept and judgment.

The conclusion of these two phrases is that apparitions of all types exist, but the apparitions, such as experiences, have a single nature, which is the primordial state. The inseparable components of the base referred to as the three primordial wisdoms are essence, nature, and energy. The essence is void, the nature is clarity, and the energy is without interruption. That is how everything manifests. All appearances that manifest have the same nature, but each single thing that manifests is also *chashe* and as a separate object. For example, energy such as *tsal* is like a crystal in a window. When sunlight touches the crystal, light of five colors appears. Through the manifestation of the crystal, the light seems like an outside object. In the same way, every single thing that manifests is part of our primordial condition. Gaining this understanding and knowledge we will be in a condition beyond concepts and dualistic judgment. If we enter into conceptual thought, we are nowhere near this knowledge. In the Dzogchen teaching, this primordial state, which is simply called the base, is our condition. In traditional Buddhism it is called the nature of mind. Thus, these two first verses explain that this knowledge of the base cannot be arrived at through concepts, but through practice.

3.2 Third and Fourth Verses

ཇི་བཞིན་བ་ཞེས་མི་རྟོག་ཀྱང་།
རྣམ་པར་སྣང་མཛད་ཀུན་ཏུ་བཟང་།

chizhinwa she mitog kyang
nampar nangdzed kuntuzang

Even though there is no thought of what is called "just as it is,"
These various appearances which are created are
   ultimately good (transcending relative good and evil).

The next lines explain the path. *Chizhinwa* is "just as it is," which means we do not create or change anything but leave things as they are. Dzogchen is said to be *chatsol tralwa*, effortless, that is, without using effort to change or create anything. *Tog* means thinking, creating something with the mind. *Mitog* means not creating, not even the concept of "as it is," because it is not by having or developing a concept that we enter into the practice of Dzogchen. For example, if somebody asks for your name and you say, "I have no name," although you really mean that you do not have a name, people will start calling you "I have no name" and this will become your name. Likewise if we use the term "as it is" and keep those words, it becomes a concept.

In the fourth line, *nampar* means all that manifests is present, nothing is missing. Some people might think that with no concept, there is nothing, everything is annihilated, so one does not have to do anything. In Dzogchen we do not have to create or change anything. As it is means how everything manifests. *Nampar* means forms or colors that manifest in *natsog*. This vision is not interrupted and everything continues as it is.

For a Dzogchen practitioner, being in the state of contemplation does not mean that our impure vision suddenly disappears, transforms, and reappears as pure vision. Having a physical human body now signifies we still have a cause to be human and thus have a human vision. We do not have to change it or get rid of it, but have to find ourselves in that understanding, in that knowledge. For example, if we know that the origin of ice is water, which comes from white light, then we would not be conditioned by the appearance of the ice. In other words, it is possible to reverse the process and go back to the origin and integrate with it. Nothing disappears and everything remains. That is what *nampar nangdzed* means.

Usually *nampar nangdzed* in Tibetan is translated as *vairochana*, which seems to be the same as the name of Buddha Vairochana. The real meaning here is that our visions are uninterrupted. Vision means not only what we see, but refers to the perception of all our senses. Everything remains present. *Kuntuzang* usually means Samantabhadra, the Buddha who symbolizes the *dharmakaya*. Here it is not the name of the Buddha. *Kuntuzang* means all-good. There is nothing to get rid of, nothing without its value. Everything is valid and everything is perfect. If we find ourselves in the nondual state with the apparition of thousands of things, *natsog*, what could be wrong? There is nothing bad about it. All-good does not refer to good as opposed to bad. We are limited by our dualistic idea of good and bad. As soon as we speak of good, immediately we think of its opposite bad, as if lurking behind good is always evil. That is not the idea.

When we say good in this way, it is not that we are rid of all evils. Rather, it means that this good is beyond the concept of good and bad. Dualism no longer exists. We have gone beyond it.

3.3 Fifth and Sixth Verses

བྱིན་པས་རྩོལ་བའི་ནད་སྤངས་ཏེ།
ལྷུན་གྱིས་གནས་པས་བཞག་པ་ཡིན།

sinpa tsolwai ned pangte
lhungyi nepe zhagpa yin

Since everything is complete in itself, abandoning the illness
    of effort,
One remains effortlessly present in the state
    of Contemplation.

These last two lines are related to the fruit. The fruit here means our attitude in this state of presence or contemplation. The fruit is not considered as a product. Saying "as it is" is already the fruit. The point is whether or not we have that understanding. *Sinpa* means accomplished from the start. *Lhundrub* means perfected from the beginning. There is nothing to be perfected. If we have the understanding of things as they are, that itself is the fruit. The problem is that we do not have that understanding. Because of our karma and our attachment, we tend to have only intellectual knowledge, which does not correspond to realization, much in the same way that even if we know ice comes from liquid water, in a frigid environment water remains solid ice.

Dzogchen Semde explains the twenty qualities of self-perfectedness, *sinpa*. If we want to examine this explanation intellectually, it might be interesting to look at these qualities one by one, but to arrive at the real meaning it is not necessary to be limited by these twenty since there could just as well be a thousand. Rather, we must understand that there is nothing to create or construct. *Sinpa* means just that.

CHAPTER THREE *Short Commentary on the Rigpai Khujug* 37

In Tantric practice, we first visualize a syllable at the heart. The syllable is said to be the potentiality of the cause. Through that cause, energy manifests and develops, and slowly our transformation becomes real. We realize the transformation almost as if we were building something. If we have an understanding of self-perfectedness, we cannot hold onto this idea, because self-perfectedness, meaning "as it is," already has that knowledge. That is why it is *sinpa*, accomplished from the beginning.

Tsolwa means commitment or effort. When speaking of *chizhinwa*, we said that it is not necessary to assume a special position or a particular way of gazing or do something particular in our existence when we do the practice. We seek to find ourselves in our condition as it is: this is what is called beyond effort. It is a characteristic manifestation of mind to think that we must make an effort or worry that we have made a mistake. What we need is to go beyond this kind of effort.

Ned means illness, *pang* means abandoned or gone beyond. *Ned pang* means that we have gone beyond that illness or disease. Disease with its characteristic effects that are never positive is always a problem. Effort, commitment, and all that one does to oneself is compared to a disease. Being beyond effort and beyond having to accomplish or construct anything, one is beyond the disease of effort and has gone beyond that problem.

Lhungyi means the condition of *chizhinwa*, as it is, the real condition, related to the condition of our body, voice, and mind. Our material body is linked to the material world, which gives rise to many problems. Knowledge and understanding of this is called *lhungyi nepe*. Without striving, without abandoning or creating anything, we effortlessly remain in the relaxed state of presence. Continuing in it, we apply the state of our body, voice, and mind in daily life. When we integrate all daily life into the continuity of the state of contemplation, that is the fruit. Everything manifests as its qualification.

The fruit of *dharmakaya*, *sambhogakaya*, and *nirmanakaya* means its qualification is manifesting as it is. When the sun is in the center of an open sky, infinite light manifests. These infinite rays of light are evidence of the quality of the sun and are its qualification. If there are clouds, these rays do not manifest. To go beyond means to go beyond the clouds into open space, and that already is the fruit. There is nothing called the fruit to construct. The only point is whether or not we have this knowledge and have integrated with the real meaning. In relation to the path, the attitude concerns integrating everything in the great contemplation. The fruit means the same thing in Dzogchen. If we want to we can analyze the three dimensions, the five dimensions, or whatever you like, but they are not something outside ourselves and are simply the same true *chizhinwa*, as it is, manifesting.

CHAPTER FOUR
Long Commentary on the Rigpai Khujug

4.1 First and Second Verses

སྣ་ཚོགས་རང་བཞིན་མི་གཉིས་ཀྱང་།
ཆ་ཤས་ཉིད་དུ་སྤྲོས་དང་བྲལ།

natsog rangzhin minyi kyang
chashe nyidu trö tang tral

Even though the nature of diversity is nondual,
In terms of individual things, it is free of conceptual
    elaborations (made by mind).

Natsog means diversity, a variety. If we have a sack filled with objects and materials, and someone asks what is in it, we can say *natsog*, many different things. In Tibetan *na* can mean nose, but in this case, *nakha* means many types. If we have numbers of objects, each slightly diverse from the other, we call them *nakha*; *tsog* means accumulated, all these things put together. In our human vision, we see things distinctly and separately like the many people and countries that exist. In every country, we have numerous places, mountains, rivers, and objects. If we go beyond the human dimension, many other situations we do not know about can be found. *Natsog* refers to the diversity of phenomena, both those we know and those we do not, including both our pure and impure visions. For example, we might think of a paradise as a luminous and wonderful place, meaning that our reference is to a pure vision at the level of the essence of the elements. On the other hand, an impure vision of an impure realm is caused by the various types of passion, a consequence of the effect of our accumulation of these passions. All of this is included in the term *natsog*, diversity. The result of so many passions, each with its particular good or bad effect, can have many outcomes that we do not know about. Through some methods of practice, a particular impure cause can be transformed into a pure one.

There are three fundamental types of vision. We generally have karmic vision, which is the effect of the principal passions such as attachment, hatred, jealousy, and pride. People who are in love start out caressing each other, but can end up stabbing each other. These are two different kinds of manifestation: stabbing is one of anger and hatred, while caressing is an expression of attachment. Nonetheless, deep down these manifestations of passion are linked. At a certain moment one may manifest more than the other, but really neither is missing.

The world of karmic manifestation is called *loka*, realm. Since passions have their characteristics, the beings from the six *lokas*, such as human, animal, and so forth, have their own characteristic visions. We all have human karma, which causes us to see things in the same way, whereas a group of mice will have the same mouse vision. An example used to explain karmic vision is as follows: six different kinds of beings meet at a river. While a human sees the river as clear and pure water, the source for a refreshing drink, for a fish the limpid water of the river is a lovely house, but for a *preta* or hungry ghost the river is molten lava that incinerates everything. Why? To see water one has to have that karmic cause. Therefore, how beings see the water depends on their individual karmic causes. We humans drink the water and it can quench our thirst, but for a hungry ghost it is liquid fire that burns them. For the gods, the river in their vision flows with exquisite nectar. A common cause produces, accordingly, a similar vision, a manifestation related to our karma. If you want to transform or change your vision, it is necessary to eliminate the cause. If not, the cause will develop and you will have to accept it. There is no other choice.

Another type of vision, called *nyamnang*, the vision of experience, is experienced by someone who is on the path of practice. When a person relaxes the elements in his or her existence or relaxes body, voice, and mind so that everything is harmonized, then experiences manifest. The manifestation does not have to be only visual, in front of our eyes. Since we have five senses, five kinds of manifestation, a visual form, a sound, or a smell can appear. Since a practitioner has senses and objects of senses, as well as myriads of passions and the energy functions of his or her condition, infinite experiences can occur. This is called the vision of experience.

Three principal *nyams* are experienced on the path: *dewa*, *salwa*, and *mitogpa*, respectively pleasurable feeling, clarity, and emptiness. But not only three types of *nyam* exist: there are thousands. The aspects of our three existences of body, voice, and mind are connected to the three principal types of *nyam*. Linked to the relaxed mind is the characteristic *nyam* of *mitogpa*, an experience of no thought, or even if thoughts arise, of not being disturbed by them. Practicing Shine, especially in the Sutra tradition, we can find ourselves in a state of emptiness. In Dzogchen that is called an experience of *mitogpa*, connected to the nature of the mind.

Another aspect of our existence is associated with the voice. If we relax our bodily energy, which is related to the five elements, the aspects and characteristics of the elements will manifest, such as apparitions of smoke, flashes, fog, lightning, or mirages, all linked to the relaxation of our energy. This is called the experience of *salwa*, clarity.

The third aspect of our existence is the physical body. When our practice of Shine is going well, at a certain moment our body seems to cease to exist or we may feel a great pleasure as if floating in space. That is connected with the body and is called the experience of *dewa*, pleasurable feeling. If we do a practice such as *kundalini*, which is connected to the physical body, the sensation of pleasure increases. We are not pretending. We really feel this experience of *dewa* because it is linked to our physical body. So we have three characteristic experiences, *dewa*, *salwa*, and *mitogpa*, related respectively to our body, voice, and mind. These three experiences are only examples; millions could be found.

In addition to karmic vision and the vision of experience, there is a third kind of vision called *tagnang*, pure vision. Purifying and eliminating all impure karmic visions does not mean that everything disappears. All visions remain, but they are now pure. For example, a Tantric practitioner transforms the five passions into five wisdoms. This is not the elimination or annihilation of passion, but their manifestation in another way. If energy exists, it continues. The famous word *gyüd*, or tantra, means continuation, which refers to the continuity of our energy. *Natsog* means the many conditions that exist, *rangzhin* the nature or inherent condition of all the infinite aspects we have just spoken about. *Minyi* means nondual, the real condition of things as they are, their true nature not being different from how they appear. This condition is the base. Our base, our actual condition, is pure, limpid, and clear, like the mirror. In this base, infinite reflections appear. Why are there reflections? Because of secondary causes. Relative conditions are linked to time and space. Of course time is not stable, but changes. When the sun is out it seems like a beautiful spring day. When it is foggy it seems that the sun does not exist. Everything is linked to time, place, and other conditions. Things that are linked to secondary causes change what we generally mean by the relative condition.

We know that thousands of reflections can arise in a mirror as a result of the conditions present in front of it. *Natsog*, diversity, is linked to all the secondary causes, which include the effects and manifestations of the real condition, but when we speak of the inherent condition, *rangzhin*, of existence as it is, at that level there are no differences among the manifestations. In the Dzogchen teaching words such as *minyi* and *nyimed*, meaning nondual, are of great importance. Union, *sungjug*, suggests that two things have been put together and somehow united. However, nonduality right from the beginning has no consideration at all of the existence of two separate things. This is the base, what we mean by the real condition of things.

The nondual condition cannot be constructed with the mind but we can understand it in practice through the teaching. Using the mind to think we have understood well is a false conclusion. We have not understood anything because the mind has entered into judgment and believes in something. Our mind and its judgments are at the relative level in time. When we enter into mental reasoning and judgment, we can observe that we are not able to think about ten things at once because the mind is limited. If we have ten matters to think about, the second one is knocking at the door but the first says, "Oh, the mind is engaged." So the mind is taken up with that and we obviously cannot think about the third or fourth thing. That means our mind is limited at the relative level of time, and this is what we generally mean by the mind being limited. If we think about nonduality, we are engaged in that moment with that thought. That is not nondual, but merely thinking about nonduality. We have to differentiate this and understand that there is real nonduality and there is *thinking* about nonduality, which are absolutely not the same thing.

Doing a practice in general and above all in the Dzogchen teaching is for acquiring a particular experience. Through experience we can enter into and develop our state of knowledge. We can also overcome certain obstacles to the state of knowledge through the various experiences in the practice. Diversity refers to all aspects of pure and impure visions, including both karmic visions and the visions of experience. Although an infinite variety of manifestations exist, their nature is said to be nondual. That is why it is important, first of all, to understand what is meant by the base, and then really enter into contemplation by doing practice; through that experience we discover what nonduality is.

Doing practice is a good way of experiencing and finding the nonduality in our impure vision. Dreams are one example. It is not so difficult to find awareness in a dream. The effect of our dream practice can be applied to our karmic vision to discover its unreality. It is more difficult to discover the unreality of our karmic vision than to discover the unreality of our dream through dream practice. In the same way, a practitioner practices in order to have different types of experience. It is not extremely difficult to enter into the understanding of nonduality through experience. What is difficult is to integrate the state of nonduality with our karmic vision; but it is not impossible. One can eventually do it and thus develop that state. That is why it is important first to understand the diversity and nonduality of everything.

When we enter into a practice, we have our experiences. For example, in Guruyoga practice, we may visualize an A in the center of our body. That is something we imagine, something we elaborate and work out with our mind. From the A light expands in all directions and the universe manifests as luminosity. We manifest in the center of this illumination. In that instant we do not think so much, but rather are present in the center of that clarity. We can remain for a long time in that presence. If we can enter into that presence, then we are present with clarity. In Tantrism, the final goal of visualizing a deity in front of ourselves or ourselves as the deity is to find the experience of being in that state of clarity. Whether we do it through visualizing a deity or visualizing light, the experience is the same. If we are in the presence of that light, that is the experience of clarity.

CHAPTER FOUR *Long Commentary on the Rigpai Khujug*

Perhaps we enter into the state of void, as if everything had disappeared and nothing is left. Even we ourselves are not there. What does that mean? There is no longer a house, there is nothing to sit on, and there is total emptiness as if in the middle of space. Thus we have another experience – that of emptiness.

Maybe we transform into a deity like Kalachakra, a joyous manifestation. In this presence, minimally, we must feel some sensation and that is the sensation of pleasure. The sensation is an experience.

Now we have found three different kinds of experience: one is clarity, one is emptiness, and the other is sensation. This, too, is *natsog*, diversity. Not only these three, but thousands of experiences can be related to ourselves. When we say nature is nondual it means that a precise presence always exists in all the different kinds of experience. Who is present in this illuminated universe? Who is present in the fear of total emptiness? Who is present in the moment of pleasure? There are differences in the experience, but there is no difference in the single presence. You must not cling to the experience, but remain in the presence. When you know that, you know the true meaning of contemplation and the meaning of nonduality.

Nonduality is our base. Rational mind does not construct it. The different aspects of our base manifest as essence, nature, and energy. This explanation also enables us to understand better what to do on the path and what the fruit is. The truth is that although the infinite aspects, *natsog*, exist, they are nondual in nature.

At the end of the phrase is the word *kyang*, meaning but, or even though. This is because if the essence of everything is nondual, we might think that everything is mixed together. The second verse starts with *chashe*. In Tibetan *cha* means part, *she* means belonging to. *Chashe* means individual parts that belong. For example, my hand is part of my body, and the finger is part of my hand. They are not independent and are neither universal nor single. In the Dzogchen teaching, the state of an individual is *chigpu*, unique, because the state of every individual is like the center of the universe. All apparitions, manifestations, and visions are aspects of the energy of the primordial state. Although they all appear singly as distinct, with each having precise functions, all are part of the energy of the individual, the manifestation of the single primordial state. Although these single things manifest with their own characteristics, the nature of the things themselves is beyond concept.

Nyid means that only a single real state exists for these things. To explain the base, we speak of energy: *tsal*, *dang*, and *rolpa*. These three aspects are a single manifestation, and that itself is beyond concept. This explanation is meant to make one understand the characteristic way energy manifests.

A crystal is often used in Dzogchen in an introduction to our primordial state because it is transparent and its nature is pure, limpid, and clear. When a secondary cause is present, an enlightened being can manifest as a deity and its mandala in relation to that cause. This is what we mean by pure vision and is part of the energy called *tsal*. If our own state is the crystal, then all that manifests as light outside comes from us, the crystal. There can be thousands of different colors and forms in the manifestation, but they all have origin in the crystal. All of that light is *chashe*; it belongs to and is part of the crystal.

It is the same for impure vision, which is produced by karma. If we accumulate much karma with many secondary causes, it will become heavier and more solid through our attachment. Everything originally manifests as light. As long as we understand that, we can have pure vision because light is the essence of the elements. Gradually, however, the light is made denser and heavier through our karma. In association with our human karma, white light becomes the element water, which we can drink to quench our thirst. According to the secondary causes that manifest, the pure elements transform. In this way, things can develop like water becoming ice. If ice melts and,

CHAPTER FOUR *Long Commentary on the Rigpai Khujug* 47

becoming water, then re-enters into white light, it is called reversing the process, reintegration. That gives an idea of energy and the process of how it manifests.

Energy also manifests as various passions. Recognizing these manifestations as part of an individual's energy, a Tantric practitioner will transform the passion into wisdom. Buddhist Sutra, however, speaks of the cessation of negativities and passions called the way of renunciation; once the causes are cut off, the effect will not manifest. When the Buddha taught, he started from the first noble truth, the truth of suffering. The second noble truth is about the cause of suffering. The third noble truth, the cessation of suffering, means that when the causes are stopped, the cause of suffering no longer exists. How does one stop suffering? There is the fourth and last noble truth, the truth of the path. These are the famous Four Noble Truths, characteristic of the way of renunciation.

It is said that a Dzogchen practitioner should not lack three qualities: *yangdaggi tawa*, *champa*, and *ngejung*. *Yangdaggi tawa* means correct point of view. The correct way of seeing in Dzogchen is to observe oneself. Until one does that, it is not the pure way of seeing. *Champa* means compassion. *Ngejung* is usually translated as renunciation, especially in the Buddhist Sutra, but actually it is not an easy word to translate. The word *ngejung* comes from *ngepar jungwa*, where *ngespar* means real, and *jungwa* indicates that one is struck by this reality and sees that this is the way. It is almost like having an impulse within oneself. There is no precise way to translate the word. Perhaps we can say that *ngejung* means participation, and this participation should not be lacking for a Dzogchen practitioner.

On the path of renunciation, *ngejung* might mean one feels disgust. One may be disgusted by the suffering of existence and renounce it. Translated as renunciation *ngejung* does not correspond to Dzogchen, which is absolutely not the path of renunciation. It would, therefore, seem strange to say that renunciation must not be lacking in Dzogchen. The same word is used, but the way of understanding it is different.

Dzogchen is said to be based on four points called *tönpa zhi*, the four bases of reliance. Without these qualities a teaching is no longer Dzogchen. The first point states:

ཆོས་ལ་མི་རྟོན་གང་ཟག་ལ་རྟོན།
chöla mitön kangzagla tön

Chö means the teaching, *kangzag* means the person interested in the teaching, and *mitön* means the principle is not based on that. In other words, this phrase means that the principle is not based on the teaching but is based on the person. This is the exact opposite of the principle explained in Tantra and Sutra:

གང་ཟག་ལ་མི་རྟོན་ཆོས་ལ་རྟོན།
kangzagla mitön chöla tön

In Tantra and Sutra, *kangzag* refers to the judgment of ordinary people, which is considered deceptive, and therefore faith has to be had in *chö*, the teaching. In the path of renunciation, a person is subordinate to the teaching because followers of Sutra have a lower capacity and are not inclined to take responsibility for themselves. That is why vows and rules set the limit for such persons' actions. If I want to do something, I first check the Vinaya rules to see whether I can do it or not. If the rules say I should not do it, I am prepared not to do it. This is what is meant by a person being subordinate to the teaching.

In Dzogchen, it is the opposite. You find out what your condition is and look at means and methods to make the most suitable decisions. Dzogchen teaching never says what a person should or should

CHAPTER FOUR *Long Commentary on the Rigpai Khujug* 49

not do. You apply different methods and by doing so discovers for yourself your own condition. It is important not to worry about the methods you use and become a slave to them. Thinking that "Ah, I have learned this practice and I must dedicate myself to it," according to Dzogchen is a mistake. Teaching depends on the person, not the other way around.

In my wardrobe I have at least twenty pieces of clothes. Some are big, some small. Some are useful when I am heavy and some when I am thin, but whether they fit me or not, I do not worry about it: they are all in my wardrobe. The same applies to the teaching. You can use all methods, even those of another tradition; you do not risk anything. If you do not understand your real condition, you will become a slave of all these methods. That is why the principle is not based on the teaching but on the person.

The second point states:

རྣམ་ཤེས་ལ་མི་རྟོན་ཡེ་ཤེས་ལ་རྟོན།

namshela mitön yeshela tön

Generally knowledge and many teachings are based on reason. *Namshe* means the knowledge of mind. The mind here means judgment. The principle is to use not the judging mind, but primordial wisdom. Wisdom arises through the transmission received from the master. The master transmits and gives the methods through whose application one discovers the true condition as it is. The characteristic of Atiyoga is the way of *rigpa*, not the mind. That is why you must find yourself in the state of contemplation from the beginning. Even the thousands of methods you might learn are all secondary and only for understanding, entering, and developing this wisdom.

The third point states:

ཚིག་ལ་མི་རྟོན་དོན་ལ་རྟོན།
tsigla mitön tönla tön

Tsig signifies words and terms and *tön* is the real meaning. You should rely not on words but on the real meaning. For example, a word like *ngejung* can be translated as renunciation although it means renunciation only in Sutra. At the level of Dzogchen, you have to know the real meaning, and that is what this *tönpa*, the third basis of reliance, says: you have to look at the real meaning and not the word.

When you discover the single state of presence in the various types of experience and manifestation, you have finally perceived the nature that is nondual. In Dzogchen this is the famed state of contemplation. If you understand what contemplation is, you know that relaxation is not an intention or commitment that says "I want to relax." The principle of relaxation is beyond any kind of tension. From that point on one relaxes everything. In Dzogchen we often use the word *lhödpa*. *Lhöd* means something loosened, relaxed. Sometimes we say *lhödpa chenpo*, total relaxation. It is not that one has to relax, but that the nature of contemplation is relaxed. That is why in Dzogchen we also say *tsolmed*, without effort, or *chatsol tralwa*, without commitment to do anything.

The Tibetan word for being in contemplation is called *chogzhag* which means not creating anything, leaving things as they are. One of the specific practices of the Dzogchen teaching is called Tregchöd. Many people think that this term Tregchöd refers to a direct path, like an airplane or a missile that arrives somewhere swiftly. You can think that if you like, but it is a mistaken idea. We think of a rocket leaving the earth at a particular point and going to a specific location, another planet. Already we have a defined notion of the place from which it is

CHAPTER FOUR *Long Commentary on the Rigpai Khujug* 51

departing and the place to which it is going whereas in Dzogchen no such concrete signposts exist, only the principle of knowledge.

Some teachings speak of various levels of teaching and attainments such as the first, second, and third *bhumis* of the bodhisattvas, and so on, which continue to rise until you reach buddhahood. This way of considering is not related to the true nondual state. That is why the name of *Dzogpa Chenpo Sa Chigpa*, the Great Perfection of only one *bhumi*, is used. *Sa Chigpa* means one single *bhumi*. You are either in the state of Dzogchen or you are not. At first the state of knowledge arises and then develops through relaxation.

The term Tregchöd does not mean going directly. *Treg* means something like a tied-up bundle and *chöd* means that which binds this bundle loosens, so that it unties itself. You should not think that this means a laid back do-nothing situation. Some people see Tregchöd as advice to do nothing and think, "Fine, I'll do nothing at all," but really the principle that needs to be integrated is what is meant by relaxing because the Dzogchen teaching is about that.

The way of seeing is understood in terms of your own experience, so that you have to, as it were, turn things around. If not looked at in that manner, how can we speak of something being nondual? If I see both a giant and a tiny child, I cannot say that the two of them are the same. Looking at this tent, we can see red and yellow stripes. We cannot say that they are nondual. In everything one finds the subject and object relationship and that is dualism, the way we as individuals, as subjects, look at objects. In Dzogchen, an explanation exists of where and how energy arises. One learns about it in theory as an idea and then enters into it in practice. Finally you can know what nondual means and understand that the way of seeing in Dzogchen does not refer to looking outward. If we always treat everything as external objects to be looked at, we cannot say that the nature of diversity is nondual because if it is nondual, why is there so much to discuss or debate? Some in accord with the Sutra system may argue that, "Its absolute nature is nondual, but relatively it is not nondual." In the Dzogchen teaching that idea of relative and absolute condition does not correspond at all. You should not have two truths like two legs to walk with, thinking, "Ah, yes, now put the relative foot forward, now put the absolute foot forward." That is dualism and as long as it is dualism, it is always the basis of transmigration.

The way of seeing in Dzogchen is like looking in the mirror and seeing your own face. Even if I do not like what I see, I have to accept it. I discover that it is my face. Slowly I discover that maybe some other existence is in the background behind that face. You can see that the direction of seeing phenomena is different. When you know how to turn things around in the direction of the mirror, you are beginning to understand something.

When a master explains that the base is more or less like this, you might think, "So, that is it," and then you hold that as a concept. That is how concepts are created if we do not understand the precise meaning of the base. We may not be aware that it is just a concept and that creating a concept is itself an obstacle. Usually we talk about the obstacles of passions and of karma as the result of bad past actions. Such hindrances can be discovered quite easily, but there is also what we call the obstacle of knowledge. This is especially consequential and damaging for practitioners, especially for those who have been on the path for a long time. In Tibetan it is called *shejai dribpa* where *sheja* is knowledge and *dribpa* is obstacle. Creating concepts produces troublesome impediments that are extremely difficult to discover. That is why the way of seeing and the understanding of the base in Dzogchen is so important.

4.2 Third and Fourth Verses

ཇི་བཞིན་བ་ཞེས་མི་རྟོག་ཀྱང་།
རྣམ་པར་སྣང་མཛད་ཀུན་ཏུ་བཟང་།

chizhinwa she mitog kyang
nampar nangdzed kuntuzang

Even though there is no thought of what is called just as it is,
These various appearances which are created are
    ultimately good (transcending relative good and evil).

4.2.1 What does "as it is" mean?

Chizhinwa means as it is, without correcting, changing, or influencing which are activities carried out by the mind. Throughout our lives, we enter into mental reasoning and analysis. Reasoning is not part of peaceful living. If you want to relax, you have to go beyond this and find yourself in your condition as it really is. This is one of the principal considerations in practice.

The fourth point says:

དྲང་དོན་ལ་མི་རྟོན་ངེས་དོན་ལ་རྟོན།
trangdönla mitön ngedönla tön

The whole phrase means do not rely on *trangdön*, what things seem to be according to what people say, but on how things really are. *Tön* (pronounced *dön* here) means meaning. *Trang* can be understood in the following way: if someone is unfriendly toward me, somehow I make him my friend. Whether it is giving him a present or by saying some pleasant words, psychologically I make him feel that he is a wonderful person. Perhaps I enter into the person's culture and habits. Although I do not smoke because I know it is bad for me, if I am with somebody who likes smoking, I might try to be congenial by lighting up a cigarette. That means I am entering into that person's habits, at least in order to communicate with him.

We know what causes the six *lokas*, each of which has its particular karmic vision. We know that Shakyamuni Buddha, for example, entered into the karmic vision of individuals in order to be able to communicate with them. He did not argue with people about what they believe at a relative level. If you have studied Buddhist philosophy such as the *Abhidharmakosha* in particular, you will know how *kham*, the universe, or *dhatu* in Sanskrit which is about a flat world with Mount Meru, the four continents, and so forth are described. Many pandits, particularly learned monks, conditioned and limited by words, think that this description expressed by Buddha is the specific Buddhist view of the cosmos. When you speak about the planet earth as round, as we do today, they say, "How can that be possible?"

When I arrived in India for the first time, I was in Kalimpong for a few months where an able and learned Mongolian *geshe* lived. This *geshe* interested me a great deal and I became a good friend of his, also because I was studying Mongolian language and literature and whenever I did not understand something I went to him. We spent much time together and sometimes we got into arguments when he would question me, saying "What do you think of this round earth business?" I would reply, "I do not think it strange. I myself believe it." His answer was, "For goodness sake, it is impossible that the earth is round. If you believe in that sort of thing you do not believe the words of Buddha." I said, "Who says that I do not believe in the Buddha's words?" He said, "Well, look at the whole *Abhidharmakosha*. The explanation is there. How could you possibly believe in a round earth?" I tried to argue a little, but felt that it was impossible, so it was better to leave him alone. I was afraid that if I argued too much, he would refuse to study Mongolian with me. A few days later, he showed me a whole exercise book where he had written his arguments disproving that the earth was round. He told me to take the book home to study what he had to say and wanted me to tell him what I thought. He was sure that if I read this book I would discover that I was mistaken. I can understand that mentality perfectly, because many people think in the same way.

The truth is that the Buddha entered into and communicated through the culture and habits of people. In the *Abhidharmakosha* the whole explanation of *dhatu*, of the universe, is typical of the culture that existed well before the arrival of Buddha in India. Buddha did not take birth to provoke a revolution in India, knowing very well that these were the concepts that were believed in. That is why he said that until final realization, everything is illusory. But if Buddha did not believe in the reality of anything and did not confirm anything, why did he choose to make the explanation in the *Abhidharmakosha*? What happened is that Buddha accepted and entered into people's understanding in order to communicate with them. *Trangdön* means to persuade people to enter into understanding by using concepts familiar to them.

In the Buddhist teachings, we speak of *trangdön* and *ngedön*. The Buddhist Sutra is the vehicle of *trangdön*, the vehicle of the cause, to carry people into understanding. Dzogchen teaching, however, is the vehicle of *ngedön*. *Ngedön* means real, the true meaning, called that because we enter into the real meaning as it is without changing anything. *Chizhinwa* means this. This is not knowledge about a final stage of meditation, but something essential to discover now.

People who study Tantrism learn a multitude of subtle definitions and when they speak about the nature of mind think that it is the final point of arrival. In Dzogchen, when we speak about *chizhinwa*, we are not only speaking about the nature of mind, we are also speaking about our existence as it is. The real understanding of the existence of our body, voice, and mind is not a conceptual idea of the nature of mind that we have to find in the state of *chizhinwa*. The knowledge of *chizhinwa* is Dzogchen itself. *Chizhinwa* must not become a concept.

In Dzogchen practice, the aspects of our body, voice, and mind must not be conditioned. This is exemplified in the text called *Dorje Sempa Namkha Che*, the Great Space of Vajrasattva, which says that if one makes any correction of the body it is no longer true Dzogchen. Another section says that remaining with spine straight and body controlled is not real contemplation, but an obstacle to contemplation. Many people from other schools therefore say that Dzogchen negates everything about meditation and control of one's posture. The problem with their immediate response that Dzogchen negates something is that people are too conditioned by the need to reject or accept things. In truth that teaching is not negating anything but rather simply giving an explanation of how to find oneself in the state as it is without correction. To find oneself in one's nature means that nature is not something that needs to be changed or has been changed. One of the fundamental terms used in Dzogchen is *machöpa*, not correcting. If one corrects something, one is working with the mind and consequently the contemplation is falsified. That is why it is said, "This is not contemplation." One must understand that finding oneself in the state of contemplation means that state is *chizhinwa*, as it is.

In the Upadesha, the way of contemplation is explained with the Four Chogzhags, remaining as it is. The first is *riwo chogzhag*, the *chogzhag* of the mountain and is related to our bodily aspect. What is the position to apply in contemplation? Simply find yourself in your condition as it is, relaxed without correction. A mountain can be high, low, wide, or of any shape. Why are some mountains pointed and high? Because of sharp pinnacles. Why should a mountain be broad and

CHAPTER FOUR *Long Commentary on the Rigpai Khujug* 57

loose? Because of boulders and earth. It is its own nature, just like that. The mountain does not have any idea of itself as high or low. Its shape is due to the secondary causes present. Human beings generally live according to secondary conditions. If it is midnight, I am usually in bed. If it is eleven in the morning, you probably can find me dressed and walking about. This is due to the secondary causes called day and night, two of the hundreds of thousands of secondary causes in existence. We do not know what the secondary causes will be at the time when we are in contemplation. If we find ourselves at the moment of contemplation in the condition of *chizhinwa*, then whatever position we are in is the position of contemplation. Enter into the slightest alteration and you create falsity. If I find myself entering into the state of contemplation lying down comfortably, and I suddenly think, "Oh, here comes contemplation. I have to jump up and sit straight," or if I am having a coffee in the kitchen and find myself in contemplation and I rush into the next room immediately and sit in position, then that is not *chizhinwa*. If we want to integrate practice well into our daily life, we have to understand this *chizhinwa*.

Integrating practice into daily life does not mean that in every moment of our life we have to be doing some formal practice. Integrating means our daily life being just as it is becomes the practice itself. This can come about when you truly understand the meaning of *chizhinwa*. The principle in the Dzogchen teaching when one speaks of contemplation is *machöpa*, not correcting. Someone might say, "Oh well, that means I cannot do anything. No Yantra Yoga,[3] no breathing, no meditation, nothing," but really you have to understand that not correcting anything is not negating anything. We are simply too habituated to yes or no. If I say something is not good, everybody takes it to mean bad. A Dzogchen practitioner should not be like this. We must be more open. We should not continue to live within our mental limits. We must learn other possibilities.

Our minds are limited by time. We can only think of one thing at a time. When we are thinking of the first subject, we cannot think of the second as well, because the mind is occupied. That is why we have so many conflicts. If we know what contemplation is, we can go beyond time, beyond the judgment of the mind, and beyond these problems. Not correcting, not creating, not influencing means you have learned not to create problems.

There is a little story about two brothers, Giorgio and Mario, who live together in a house. In that house are only these two brothers and nobody else. In another place are many families and all the people there know Giorgio and Mario. One day, some friends of Giorgio and Mario go to their house to visit them, but while they are approaching, they see Mario going to the market. So they know that Mario is not at home, but think Giorgio may be at home. Of course, Giorgio may not be there either. When the friends get near the brothers' house, they hear someone playing a flute. They think, "So Giorgio is at home," because they know only these two live there. They do not know of a third person. When they knock on the door and it opens, someone they have never seen before appears. They are surprised that it is not Giorgio.

Similarly, we are limited by always seeing things in our habitual way which comes about through the constraints of our mind and its reasoning. Furthermore, the mind reasons with the help of our senses. Our sense faculties, like seeing with the eyes and listening with the ears, are all inadequate. A limited mind with the five limited senses is like a person with five very limited friends. This little group of five or six sets out without the ability to establish any fact and cannot understand the real conditions. That is how we usually reason: yes or no, it is or it is not. This is called the manifestation through the mind. Going beyond this is what we called *chizhinwa*, not correcting, without changing anything.

In the Dzogchen teaching, we have no need to say, "I belong to this school," or "I belong to this way of seeing." Nothing changes in the least whether or not you feel or say that you are a Buddhist. Doing so is already a limit, a mistake. One has to understand one's own condition in order to be able to open oneself. Many of you may have heard of the Rimed school of non-sectarianism. Many people say, "Ah, there is this wonderful Rimed, non-sectarian school." From the point of view of Dzogchen, I am not at all amazed by the Rimed School. Even the idea of nonsectarianism is limited. Rimed is a name used by someone to describe something in confines set by that person even though this is not its way of being. The primordial condition is explained as manifesting as essence, nature, and energy. These are called the three primordial wisdoms, but are terms used only for those who are limited. We are limited, so we say that the basic condition of the individual is the essence, nature, and energy. Although it seems concrete, that analysis has nothing to do with the primordial condition and how it is. Such an analysis is false, but nevertheless there is some truth in it because we find ourselves in the relative condition. The explanation is done relatively, appropriate to our condition. However, it does not mean that it corresponds to the way things really are.

A nonsectarian school means that the people who are its members are not limited by sectarianism, but also here that term does not correspond to the true condition of things. For example, Jamyang Khyentse Wangpo and Jamgön Kongtrul Rinpoche are said to be the masters who founded this nonsectarian school. It is not that they sat down and said, "Yes, we want to found a school which is nonsectarian." When the sun rises in space, it is inevitable that infinite light beams out. The sun does not say, "Look, my rays are shining." The rays themselves do not enter into the confines of saying, "This is wonderful brilliant sunshine." Rather it is those who enjoy the sunlight and see it, those who were in the dark, who say that the sun is shining. When we speak about the nonsectarian school, we are really referring to the manifestation of those masters and practitioners.

One of the principal masters involved and usually associated with the nonsectarian movement was Jamyang Khyentse Wangpo. He was a great Dzogchen master and he came from the Sakyapa School. Another is Jamgön Kongtrul who came from the Kagyüdpa School, and Paltrul Rinpoche who was from the Nyingmapa School. They were all Dzogchen practitioners. This is the way of manifesting the view of Dzogchen in practice, but none of them announced that they had a nonsectarian school. People thought of these masters in this way but this does not mean that was an accurate description.

We need to understand the importance of this point. For a Dzogchen practitioner, it is not necessary to publicize that, "We belong to the nonsectarian school." If we speak of nonsectarianism, it means you can come to my place, but it is my place. If I close my door, you cannot come in. I will not shut the door in your face and you can come to my house in a friendly way. However, it is clear that if you come to my house, you must not disturb me. You have to respect my condition, this idea of you and me, your position and my position. If you and I exist, that is plural, and from this plurality arise others as well. Naturally ideas such as nonsectarianism will occur.

By saying nonsectarian, we are simply admitting and confirming that sects exist. Even though we recognize and accept the existence of sectarianism, it does not mean that the circumstance that leads to it is valid. Claiming to be non-sectarian means we ourselves have that same sectarian position. If we have that way of thinking, it is already a mistake. In Dzogchen it says,

gyached chog lhung tralwa

རྒྱ་ཆད་ཕྱོགས་ལྷུང་བྲལ་བ།

Gyarma chedpa means not falling into limits; *chog lhung tralwa* means if we fall into limits, we are working with the mind and will continue to transmigrate. If we are not within such limits, we are in wisdom. That is what is meant by limitation and going beyond limitation. The real meaning is not only a mental consideration but corresponds to our body, voice, and mind. Thus *chizhinwa* means beyond limits, as it is.

In Dzogchen you have to integrate everything. You have to remove the barrier of you and me and understand the real condition as it is. This is called *chizhinwa*, in which no barrier exists. That is fundamental. When you have really learned the meaning of the absence of a barrier, you know the way to relax tension. If we find the way to relax our tensions, we are in contemplation.

The fourth verse says, "Do not interrupt any object of the senses." It is unlike the principle in Tantrism where you transform impure visions into pure visions. There is nothing to transform because transformation itself is a concept. This is a path of self-liberation and nothing is to be transformed or created by the mind. Whatever appears is simply present and is called clarity in Dzogchen. Anything that belongs to clarity is just that. Nothing is bad.

We see this tent now in which we are seated. Logically this is our karmic vision because we have our common human karmic vision. This is not a pure vision, but it is not necessary to change it into a tent of light because doing that would be playing with the mind. Even if the tent belongs to our karmic vision, it is still part of our clarity. If I say to myself, "This is a beautiful tent. Perhaps we need to buy a big tent like this," it is reasoning. Reasoning means we have entered into the judgment of the mind which is the cause of karma and all that karma creates.

In the practice of Chöd, for example, Machig Labdrön explained that the first demon is *wangpo thogchekyi düd*. *Wangpo* means the senses. The something that blocks the clarity in these senses is said to be one of the demons. What does this mean? Seeing something beautiful, we not only see it, we immediately think,

"How beautiful," and "I really want that." That is a desire which is a passion. Following that, one creates an action and the mind enters into judgment. How did that thought arise? First the eyes saw that beautiful object. That is not so bad, but a blocking or stopping of this perception follows, and the mind begins creating thoughts. When such a block happens, we call it a demon. If nothing is blocked, in Dzogchen it is said to be like a snake which ties itself in a knot and then unwinds itself. Something of great beauty may arise, but I do not make the judgment "I want it" or "I like it," and that not entering into mental judgment is clarity. Whether something is beautiful or ugly, there is no difference between them. Everything is present while the mind is not functioning, and that is the state of *chizhinwa*. One is present in contemplation, a state not to be confused with the mind which judges and desires.

Nampar nangdzed means that none of the apparitions is changed or transformed with no distinction between good and bad in whatever arises. One finds oneself present in the state of *rigpa* where everything is an ornament. That is why it is said to be *kuntuzang*, all good. How do you apply this *chizhinwa* in practice? In Dzogchen using methods to have experiences in order to arrive at *chizhinwa* is fine, but you must not confound this as a principal issue.

Let us take the example of Tantrism. The principle of Tantrism is transformation. A limited form or method of transformation is contained in a particular Tantra such as Hevajra, although there are numerous others. This method is for transmitting knowledge through transformation. In this case, the realized individual who has set out to transmit the knowledge through transformation is called Hevajra. His dimension, function, wisdom, and all that manifests are called the mandala. Through this means, one receives the transmission of knowledge. One who has received such transmission sets out to apply it. Every day that individual transforms himself into the dimension of Hevajra, reciting mantras and trying to integrate his state of energy into the transformation. In this way, at a certain moment of manifestation which represents clarity, everything is integrated into this clarity and one enters into the state of contemplation. This is called Mahamudra, the Great Symbol. An individual to bring about this transformation in Tantrism must continue repeating the practice. This method becomes an important path.

This method clearly differs greatly from that of *chizhinwa*, of not correcting. In the Nyingmapa tradition, higher yoga is analyzed into three levels: Mahayoga, Anuyoga, and Atiyoga. Mahayoga is the path of gradual transformation and Anuyoga is the path of nongradual transformation, both being paths of transformation. On those two paths, until you find yourself in the state of contemplation in clarity, the method used throughout is always transformation. That method which is not considered important in Dzogchen is the principal method in Tantrism. However, arriving at Mahamudra, the final point of Tantrism, one sees that the method used to reach the final point was not in itself the principle. You can understand this if you read the *dohas*, the songs of the *mahasiddhas*, or their stories. Related to the Hevajra Tantra, for example, is the story of Virupa who was one of the great masters. Virupa was a studious Indian pandit who became a practitioner of Tantrism. For years and years he did the transformation practice of Hevajra. In order to transform his energy, he practiced the mantra of Dagmema, the *yum* or female aspect of Hevajra, for years and years. One day in the clear state of total contemplation, he picked up the mala that he had been using for mantra recitation and threw it in the toilet. The mandala that he had prepared for practice was also thrown away and he left. Everyone said, "He has gone mad." It is true that realized beings often appear a little crazy. In fact, they are not the crazy ones, we are, deranged by all our passions and attachments. We do not recognize our madness, always thinking that it is others who are a bit daft.

People in their real condition as it is without correcting or changing anything may seem crazy. When you find yourself in this state, the final point in Tantrism, you break the rules and methods by which you arrived. Now you no longer consider transformation as the main method although while you are applying the method of transformation, knowing that it is not the principle is not so important. On the contrary, if you do not have at least a minimal faith or belief in the method you are working with, you will not carry it out. That is why so much importance is given it in Tantrism right to the end.

Atiyoga is a different path from the beginning. It is not a path of transformation, but a path of self-liberation. A principle of self-liberation can exist only if one enters into a certain state of knowledge. Finding oneself in the state of knowledge is not a result of a mental decision that "I do not want to change anything." Making such a decision is called the creation of a falsification. Rather, you must discover something, the only true method for which is to know the real condition of things as they are. Practice itself is that. In the Dzogchen teaching, one explains the meaning to make another person understand, and that is called transmission. It is not necessary to prepare a mala, to have a thangka,[5] or for the teacher to use a vase to touch or pour water over someone's head. That is a different kind of transmission called initiation in Tantrism. Many people who have received an initiation through some kind of ritual think they have received the teaching, but are not satisfied if they only hear an explanation of the real meaning of the *Rigpai Khujug*. If one has not understood well, one can even think that one has not received the refuge.

4.2.2 *Refuge, Guru Yoga, Samaya*

Some people say, "I have not taken refuge; I have only listened to the Dzogchen teaching." This is a strange idea if you think about it. If

CHAPTER FOUR *Long Commentary on the Rigpai Khujug* 65

you believe you have not yet taken refuge, what have you been doing learning Dzogchen? That is the real refuge although it is not the refuge of reciting "Namo Buddhaya, Namo Dharmaya, Namo Sanghaya" in front of the statue of Buddha. Buddha said in the Sutra that the ultimate refuge is in the *tathagata*, the buddha within oneself that one has to realize. Refuge is not being satisfied simply by going to a master who gives you a new name and snips some of your hair. That can be satisfactory for someone not capable of grasping more than that level, but really not for those with the qualities and characteristics of a human being.

The Buddhist teaching states that the characteristics of a human being are thinking, reasoning, and talking. If one has those capacities and is looking for a path, one must have or develop the capacity of knowing what to look for and go beyond the idea of ritual as an answer.

It is important to know the meaning of refuge in the Buddhist Sutra, because those interested in Buddhism these days talk about refuge. Some people take refuge to receive a name so that they can feel Buddhist. It is fine if you have no other idea to begin with. However, you should not think that saying "I am a Buddhist" is the path. More important is to understand why you are doing it. Any vow you have undertaken to carry out implies that you do not have enough self-control, and that you have inferior capacity. In the Dzogchen teaching, the point is not deciding whether a person's capacity is inferior or superior. It is simply about discovering for oneself one's own capacity, not a decision made by someone else, and is related to every single individual in that it is linked to each person's personal circumstances, also depending on what each person considers as capacity and what it is used for. Circumstances are not static or fixed but are something we can change and improve. For example, in meeting a master we must have the capacity to communicate. We must at least be able to ask about what we want to find out. When the teacher is teaching and explaining, we need the capacity to understand and be able to integrate that knowledge in ourselves. These are called capacities. We practice using numerous methods of purification because we have many obstacles that hinder our capacity to understand the meaning of the teaching. If I know that I lack a certain capability, I concentrate on purification of its blockage.

You have to discover for yourself what you need. Many people go to a master with great faith and trust, thinking that the master knows everything about them. They ask, "What is my capacity?" Those who have some idea of Tantrism ask, "To what Buddha family do I belong?" An easygoing master who likes first of all to make people happy may say that they have superior capacity, or that they belong to the Buddha family or the Ratna family. Such people will be satisfied, deciding that master is fantastic. This is not a true way of responding. A master has to enable you to find out what your capacity is. All that is related to you, not the master. Sometimes the master simply by seeing or talking to the person, coming into contact, can discover his or her capacity. In that case, he can give some advice, but that is not the same as the master deciding and your following everything he decrees. He gives an idea, a method to enable you to open yourself, to make it possible for you to find out what your own condition is. He will never advise you to do one thing and not another. If he does, he is not giving a Dzogchen teaching.

If you do not know what your capacity is and you follow a teaching without the minimal understanding, what you follow becomes more of a teaching from Buddhist Sutra. In this case you have to take a vow and follow a path of renunciation. The master will set some limitations for you, and give you rules of what you can and cannot do. This is called receiving a vow from a master, and you follow everything it specifies. There is no universal vow because a vow has a certain number of rules that exist according to circumstances. Since infinite secondary causes produce an infinite number of situations, there cannot be a set of universal rules. Rather the limits set by the rules are according to the most relevant and necessary ones at a certain time.

Take the example of Vinaya, the monastic rules and see how they came about. This is the teaching the Buddha gave at the Hinayana[6] level. At the beginning, a group of monks called the *sangha* surrounded Buddha Shakyamuni. No rules existed at that time. The Buddha was the master and the monks the followers. The Buddha, when he noticed something amiss, would say, "Do not do that." For example one day some monks went naked somewhere. The next day a rule was added to the Vinaya which said, "Monks should not go around naked." After that none of them would appear naked because this had become the rule. Some monks, perhaps, were not happy about this because it was hot in India, so they tucked up their robe a bit like a miniskirt. Buddha then said the robe could not be that short but had to have a certain length, and another rule was born. Later when some ran about wearing the robe wrapped around them a rule arose saying that Buddha's monks should not run, but should walk slowly. Gradually there arose 253 rules. Unfortunately Buddha manifested his death at the age of eighty-one, so there was no time to add more rules. If Buddha had lived to be 150 years old, certainly there would have been not 253, but perhaps 1200 rules, because man is capable of doing many things and circumstances are infinite. Since the Buddha was no longer present and no one could replace him, that was the end of the creation of the Vinaya.

After that, even though some conditions did not correspond to those of Buddha's time and place, if they resembled the ideas in the Vinaya, they were still included. When the monks started obeying Vinaya rules in Tibet, many of the rules laid down in India did not correspond to the situation there. For example, it is hot in India, so the robes of the monks did not have a top half, but only a scarf. They had to wear something: walking about like this in Tibet, they would have died of cold. Thus they adopted a form of what the nuns wore in India because if the nuns walked around topless like the monks, people would have talked. So the Buddha said that they had better cover themselves. Men did not have that problem and thus remained the same. How were the nuns going to dress? Buddha took his example from the head of the elephant and suggested two flaps that come down a little like the elephant's ears. This is now worn by all Tibetan monks and nuns. That is how things develop, showing that whatever the rules are, they cannot correspond to every single situation. A person does not need rules if he has the capacity to control and be responsible for himself. For example a Tantric or Dzogchen practitioner does not have to follow the Vinaya rule. Above all in Dzogchen, it is most important to be responsible for oneself. That is why a master says, "Open yourself." Opening yourself, you see and you understand. If I am a blind man, I cannot see where I am going. I depend on a dog to lead me or somebody to help me along. It would be much better if somehow I could open my eyes, rather than depending on others to lead me. We have to open our eyes and all our senses in order to understand. The *Rigpai Khujug* explains *chizhinwa* is about how to be, leaving everything as it is. It is important to know the way of understanding and not to make mistakes. One must not confuse oneself, because usually we complicate things even when they are simple. This happens when people do not know how to discover themselves.

For example some follow a teaching by concentrating on only the minute details. If asked to sit in the lotus position, they worry about where the feet should go or how the back is to be positioned. Giving such attention to these minutiae makes them feel important because they show how many relative matters they know. In the case of a method of practice, for example, hundreds of slight variations can be found. Giving trifles such importance indicates they do not comprehend the real meaning of what they are doing. A person who follows a teaching, particularly Dzogchen, must not lose sight of the important principles offered by the master by getting involved in details in this way. If we

CHAPTER FOUR Long Commentary on the Rigpai Khujug

talk about contemplation, a principle of how to find oneself in that state is explained, but the way of sitting, the way of gazing, and the way of breathing are all relative. Relative things are secondary. One applies and uses them when necessary, but they are not indispensable.

One of the most important things in Dzogchen is Guruyoga. One might find it strange that it is not explicitly mentioned in the *Rigpai Khujug*, but Guruyoga is related to the transmission and not necessarily talked about separately. In the case of *chizhinwa*, how one has received this transmission and how one applies this contemplation is in itself Guruyoga. Guruyoga does not necessarily mean an external form. It exists when one has knowledge of this profound understanding. If a master or more than one has awakened that knowledge in the disciple, that transmission is inseparable from that master or masters and the knowledge itself is the real Guruyoga. Visualizing a marvelous master in front of myself so that I can receive light and wisdom from him is not the real Guruyoga. That would be just a practice in Yogatantra. In Yogatantra we visualize an enlightened being or bodhisattva in front of us, inviting him to send us his light in order to purify ourselves and receive his wisdom. This is a kind of Guruyoga but not the essential point and not the Guruyoga of Dzogchen. We may visualize Padmasambhava as the union of all the masters in front of us and from that figure we receive light, the transmission, and so forth. This is a relative Guruyoga, not a real Guruyoga. The real practice is the unification of the master's state of understanding and one's own state. The master has transmitted the knowledge and this understanding has arisen in us, meaning something we can actually develop. If that is not the case, the base, the principle of Guruyoga, is lacking. If one has nothing within oneself to develop, even though one has great devotion and makes invocations to the Buddha or Padmasambhava, that is all there is: devotion and invocations.

If we do Guruyoga visualizing and invoking a figure such as Padmasambhava, we should not have the idea that he is there only as a holy being called Padmasambhava. Instead, he is present as the union of all the masters. We may have ten or twenty masters. Some of them are more important because they have reawakened us at a certain point, while some are less important. However they are all related to the transmission and I am in the presence of the union of all these masters in the figure of Padmasambhava. That manifestation of Padmasambhava is also Guru Padmasambhava himself because he is in our lineage of transmission and considered a supreme body of light. Thus making use of his figure has also to do with Padmasambhava himself as an individual master, but above all, he is seen as the union of all our own masters. This is not sufficient for a student who out of pride wants to go straight to the top in order to have a direct link with Padmasambhava because he is so elevated. He might want to get in touch with Padmasambhava or Buddha Shakyamuni, the supreme figures, instead of the master from whom he received the teaching complaining that his master, just like him, eats spaghetti, goes to the toilet, and so forth. Deep down we all have this habitual way of seeing because the human karmic cause is pride and no one is lacking in it. That is why Buddhism utilizes so many prostrations, to diminish this a bit. Even if one wants to have a direct link with Padmasambhava or Buddha Shakyamuni, it is immensely difficult to achieve that. To have a link with Padmasambhava, one has to recognize one's own master as Padmasambhava.

In the Buddhist Sutra *Prajnaparamita Abhisamayalankara*, there is a sentence:

Nyimai wözer rab tsa yang

ཉི་མའི་འོད་ཟེར་རབ་ཚ་ཡང་།

meshel medpar me mijung

མེ་ཤེལ་མེད་པར་མེ་མི་འབྱུང་།

CHAPTER FOUR *Long Commentary on the Rigpai Khujug*

which means that even though the rays of the sun are powerful, without the concentrating power of a lens, you cannot light a fire. Even though thousands of buddhas are full of wisdom, you cannot receive their wisdom if it had not been communicated to you by a living master. Thus while in Sutra having a master is considered important, in Dzogchen it is considered absolutely indispensable.

However, the ways of seeing the master in Sutra, Tantra, and Dzogchen are slightly different. In Sutra, the master is regarded very much as a physical presence. In Tantrism, the importance of the master is his activity. In Dzogchen the principle is the transmission of knowledge, the unification of our state with that of the master. The *Rigpai Khujug Tantra* says that one enters into the knowledge called *chizhinwa*, the knowledge of knowing one's own state as it is, and develops it through contemplation by having received a transmission from the master. The value of the master is like *nagtsur*, a mineral used for cleaning gold. If the gold does not manifest its own color, rubbing the mineral on it will cause its gold color to appear. The example in the *Rigpai Khujug* compares the master to this mineral. The gold is called Dzogchen, our real condition, the primordial state which is self-perfected from the beginning. Our real state does not manifest due to our conditioning, our obstacles, and our confusion, similar to a nugget of gold which looks a bit red or dark yellow or like a stone or a piece of iron. When we do not possess the knowledge that our true state is like gold, it is said we suffer from *marigpa*, ignorance. The power of transmission causes us to discover our essential nature through the master. He is like the mineral that rubbed on gold enables the quality and the color of the gold to emerge. That is why Guruyoga is not considered separately in the *Rigpai Khujug*.

Remaining in the state of *chizhinwa*, the state of contemplation, is Guruyoga. That is everything. If you speak of Guruyoga, that is what Guruyoga is. If you speak of refuge, that is the supreme refuge. Until one is in that real true condition, any refuge is temporary, provisional. If you are most familiar with the Sutras, you believe that practice has something to do with the body, such as sitting in a controlled posture, purifying with movements like prostrations or through the recitation of mantras, or meditating, mentally creating deities. We are accustomed to think of these activities as practice. That is not to say that they are not practices, but of a different kind than in the Dzogchen teaching where one second in the state of *chizhinwa* is real practice and indeed the supreme practice.

We also often speak of *tamtsig*, *samaya* or promise. When you receive a Tantric teaching, an initiation, you will be told that today you have received an initiation and must promise to apply the method of transformation at least once a day. If you cannot manage to do the long transformation practice, you do a simpler version. In order to integrate that transformation into your own energy, you must recite the mantra at least seven or twenty-one times a day. An aspect of Tantrism, many other relative *samayas* of this kind exist.

That which is called *samaya* in Tantrism is called a vow in Sutra, for example one takes a vow of not drinking. When some individuals see a glass of wine, they immediately become frightened as if without great care, they might transgress and drink that wine. As if overtaken by the power of the alcohol, they run away from it in order to keep their heavy commitment to the vow. These are examples of vows and *samayas*.

In the Dzogchen teaching to find oneself in the state of *chizhinwa* is the *samaya*. The master helps you to understand that finding yourself relaxed in the state of *chizhinwa* is the real condition. Everything else, judging or creating with the mind and entering into limits, is false, unreal. The master does not tell you to abandon your real condition and falsify as much as possible. On the contrary, he will try to make you understand the relative condition and that the real condition is to find oneself in the state of *chizhinwa*. At any moment of awareness, try to find yourself in that state or when you are distracted, gradually little by little notice that you are distracted.

What does being distracted mean? Usually we think that distraction means we pay attention to something here and do not notice something else happening there. That is one kind of distraction, but that is not the only type. Here distraction is the mind and that which the mind creates to which we pay total attention. When we are in the state of contemplation, many thoughts arise but we do not follow them, almost as if we have become a watchman who notices everything that is going on around us. In that moment, we are not distracted because we notice everything that is happening. This is called presence. The state of *chizhinwa* is, therefore, the continuity of finding oneself in this presence. It does not mean eliminating or blocking anything. Distraction is when we are not present but are judging, thinking, and following thoughts as they occur. The *samaya* of Dzogchen is not to be distracted and that is all there is. When we are distracted, that does not mean we have broken our *samaya*. *Samaya* is the attempt not to be distracted, which is also how practice and Guruyoga can be identified.

There are two ways of trying not to be distracted. One way is to develop one's capacity of contemplation and gradually integrate everything into that presence. The final point for a Dzogchen practitioner is called *tingedzin khoryug chenpo*, the Great Contemplation. This way of not being distracted implies great capacity for contemplation. Capacity here means the ability to apply and develop this nondistraction. Until one has developed that, another way of not distracting oneself works with the mind. Working with the mind here does not mean to judge or create anything, but rather to have a minimal degree of attention and pressure in order not to be distracted. Any tension is always linked to the mind. Although pressure is not the goal, nevertheless it is useful for developing the capacity of nondistraction in contemplation. One pays a little attention in order not to be distracted. A feeling of being slightly pressured is created, but without charging oneself too much, otherwise the opposite result will be achieved. Droning "I must not be distracted" constantly turns the situation into a struggle, and you will become nervous. That is why in the midst of tension, some relaxation must be present in order to make the pressure a positive help for contemplation.

Take an example from normal daily life, saying to yourself, "I think I am going to go out now." That is a thought. As that thought arises, I can recognize it as such, because I know I am thinking that I want to go out. With this recognition, the thought is not blocked, nor has it disappeared. It simply continues. Now the principle is that I do not want to be distracted. I maintain this attention while also relaxing internally. I get up and go out. While I am out and when I return, I try always to pay attention and be present. That is an important practice. We are not talking about a position or anything complicated, simply walking, moving a bit, doing whatever, but trying to be present in it. It is not so easy in the beginning, but not that difficult either. Anything can be learned. Once learned, it becomes easy. First one learns it with movement, then one learns with the voice.

When I am talking to people, reasoning and thinking with my mind, I can talk for an hour or two without being distracted. What does this mean? All the aspects of body, voice, and mind can be integrated into that state. Many ask how that can be possible. How can I do that if I have to think? I think with my mind, but my mind is like a reflection in a mirror. It does not mean that I have to ignore the pure, clear, and limpid quality and capacity of the mirror. It does not mean that I am dualistically outside the mirror and someone else is observing the reflection. I can also be the mirror and have the capacity to reflect.

That is why the fourth *tönpa*, the agreement of meaning, says the principle is not mind but wisdom. Wisdom means the state of *rigpa*, presence. The presence of *rigpa* is a state beyond mind. Beyond the mind does not mean that the mind has nothing to do with it. What is the relationship between the clarity, purity, and limpidity of the mirror and the reflections? The capacity of the mirror is beyond the reflections because the reflections are dependent on what is in front of the mirror. A beautiful flower in front of the mirror will reflect a flower. If a pig is there, a pig will be reflected. Beautiful or ugly, whatever is put in front of the mirror will manifest as a reflection, relatively distinguished by its color or form. One cannot say that that which is reflected is the totality of the nature of the mirror, nor that because the nature of one's reflection is beyond the reflection, the reflection is not included.

To reflect is the nature of the mirror. It does not matter if the mirror reflects a pig or a flower, something beautiful or ugly. The principle is that it reflects. If one is ignorant of the capacity of the mirror and is at the level of dualism, then one is outside the mirror looking at the reflection, unaware of the nature of the mirror. That is the difference between the meaning of ignorance and of the state of *rigpa*. The state of *rigpa* and the mind are, therefore, two different things. For one who does not know the real condition, there is always subject and object, and of course I like to see a flower but dislike seeing a pig. At the moment one is in the state of the real condition or tries to be in that state. That is all that is necessary in Dzogchen. You do not have to sit with eyes closed or open or whatever. Rather, wherever you are, try to be in that presence and not distracted. In this way you develop through practice and can integrate it in the state of *chizhinwa*.

4.2.3 The Practice

The practice in Dzogchen Semde begins with the fixation on an object such as the letter A. One then goes on to fixate without an object. Gradually one is brought into a state of calm or Shine. The *Rigpai Khujug* has no specific explanation of how one arrives at contemplation through fixation. You can use this method if you wish, but with regard to practice, the *Rigpai Khujug* says to find oneself in the state of *chizhinwa*, being present is required. In a state of presence, without changing or altering the position of the body, the voice, or the mind, one relaxes. Relaxing does not mean allowing yourself to become drowsy. You should not feel faint. The senses are perfectly present, and the presence of the functions of the senses signifies clarity. This is what is meant by contemplation. We relax in this condition. In order to know whether we are in the state of *chizhinwa* or not while relaxing, we can examine an explanation of how the various experiences manifest.

4.2.3.1 Yowai Nyam

The first experience is called *yowai nyam*, the experience of movement. The practitioner seems to observe that thoughts increase. One may wonder how practicing a calming meditation like Shine, one can become more agitated. What happens is that at the same time we are not correcting or creating anything nor controlling the bodily position or breathing, we are relaxing in a state of presence. The fact is that the movement we notice is not an increase of mental activity but that thoughts already there are manifesting. Since the moment of birth, we have been charging ourselves with reasoning, thoughts, and all our confusions. Even if we start to think about doing a practice, we immediately worry about what we should do, what ought to happen now, what will happen next, am I making a mistake, and so it continues. We seem to know only how to create worries for ourselves. Not only do we work ourselves up now, but we have upset ourselves already, arriving actually at infinite confusion. Since we are already so confused, we do not even notice our state.

When I would go to faculty meetings at the university, all the professors present smoked at least one cigarette, some of them two.

CHAPTER FOUR *Long Commentary on the Rigpai Khujug*

The windows were all shut, because in Naples if the windows in the conference room remain open, the street noise made hearing anything else impossible. Those who did not smoke, obliged to inhale the smoke of the other professors, were disturbed by the closed windows even more, whereas the smokers of multiple cigarettes were perfectly comfortable. Similarly, because we are so harassed by ourselves, we no longer know that we are in such a state. We do not notice that we have so much mental confusion and movement in our mind. The moment we begin to relax, such movement becomes visible. Suddenly we notice how confused we are and think that the confusion is being developed by us at that moment. On the contrary, we are just beginning to notice the manifestation of our situation. Up until this point, we have been too agitated and involved in our mind to notice it. Now we are like an agitated well that, allowed to stand still, slowly becomes clear. Inside this well are frogs, fish, insects, and worms. These creatures were there before but we did not see them because the water was stirred up. As the water settles down, we can see them all. In the same way, we notice the movement of our mind because we are relaxed. That is why the experience of *yowa*, movement, manifests.

What must you do when many such movements are present? The only thing to do is to relax internally. Relax even the slightest tension. Pay no attention to the movement of thoughts. If you charge yourself, that means you are distracted. If I see somebody and think, "How disagreeable he is," it is because I am distracted: I think that I am here, he is there, he is disagreeable. If I am not distracted but simply present, I think I am here, he is there, why is he disagreeable? Even if he seems so, it does not matter because his attitude does not affect me. That is why whatever movement occurs is of no importance if one is internally relaxed. In this method of the Rigpai Khujug the only thing to do when there is any movement is to relax. This is called to relax or *chizhinwa* without directing attention.

Relaxing does not mean thinking of relaxing. Relaxing internally means you should know what is happening but not get disturbed by it. Observe if you have any tension. If there is, let it go, but do not fall sleep: remain present and relax. Do not do this practice for a long time because we are used to having an extremely agitated mind. Do this a short time, then let yourself be distracted a little as is your usual habit. Repeat this process many times. This is the way to begin the practice of *chizhinwa*.

Do not take any particular practice position since *chizhinwa* is like the first *chogzhag*: any position is fine. In Tantrism, for example, through control of the breathing, one controls the mind, but in the practice of *chizhinwa* in the *Rigpai Khujug*, the breathing should come naturally with no necessity to control anything. Just remain in this state of relaxed presence.

4.2.3.2 The Two Defects of Practice

Chingwa and *göpa* are the two main defects which often arise during practice. *Chingwa* means that through relaxing, you become sleepy. You want to do some contemplation, but after a few seconds, you fall asleep. This is called *chingwa*. On the other hand, if you want to do some contemplation but cannot succeed because you are agitated, this is called *göpa*. These two defects are respectively due to two different secondary causes. Secondary causes are linked to circumstances, such as if you have eaten a heavy meal with a bottle of good wine and you are relaxed in a warm place, you will certainly feel drowsy. On the other hand if you have many thoughts and movements, *göpa*, agitation, will arise in you.

If you know how to relax internally with presence, you can overcome the movement of agitation easily. If you wish, you can practice in a quiet place in silence for a while. You can also do this practice during certain activities, such as walking, by relaxing internally. Generally speaking, however, since we are often nervous and confused, we should start this practice in a quiet place. Those with greater capacity who are more advanced in the practice and are able to integrate more successfully can also do it in the midst of confusion. A Dzogchen practitioner is not somebody who needs to escape to a mountaintop or hide in a cave like a marmot.

An aspect of Dzogchen practice called the *chogzhag* of vision includes what we see with the eyes as well as the perception of other senses. We can remain quietly in a room without even a fly buzzing. We may be listening to beautiful classical music, nerve-racking rock music, or some terrible noise like that of a factory or a railway station. These different types of sounds are also part of our vision. We also have our other senses, such as that of smell. We may enjoy the delicate scent of a rose or some wonderful French perfume or try to avoid the odor rotten garbage or the stench of manure in the countryside. These are all called visions related to our senses of sight, hearing, smell, and so forth, and we have good, bad, or neutral relationships with them. When one is in the *chogzhag* of vision, which is also the state of *chizhinwa*, these visions are said to be ornaments of one's own state. The second verse of the *Rigpai Khujug* calls these ornaments *chashe*, part of the manifestation of the primordial state, with nothing to accept or reject because this is the condition of things as they are. One who integrates in this state is in the state of contemplation.

4.2.3.3 Thobpai Nyam

The *thobpai nyam*, the experience of obtainment, means that although movement is arising, nevertheless we continue to relax. When we are able to remain in this presence, we can continue for a long time. If you are not thoroughly present, it is easy to be disturbed again, but if you are present and are internally relaxed, you can succeed in continuing. Finding yourself in this condition is called the *thobpai nyam*. What should you do? In the *Rigpai Khujug*, no explanation of how or what one should do exists. You have to understand the characteristics of the experience, then apply and develop the practice. What has to be done is to find a way of integrating your practice in daily life.

Practically speaking, we can categorize the experiences in two types. The first is the experience of *yowa*, movement. Movement of thoughts arises when we relax. We do not need to find an antidote or to carry out a transformation. Instead, we know the condition of things and relax internally without going to sleep or losing presence. The experience of movement is practiced by relaxing in the state of presence. Continuing in the state of *chizhinwa*, you may succeed for a long time. You still need a certain commitment to continue in presence, otherwise you might fall into the defects of drowsiness or agitation. Managing to continue in this way, you will find the experience of obtainment. Following that, something else can be improved. These experiences are still almost entirely at a relative level.

4.2.3.4 An Account of Five Experiences cited in Dzogchen Semde

The *Rigpai Khujug* is a short text which does not have a long explanation as found in Dzogchen Semde. What follows is an account of five experiences generally cited in Dzogchen Semde, valid here as well.

4.2.3.4.1 The First Nyam

The first experience is said to be like a waterfall. A waterfall is in constant movement and makes a clamorous sound as the water strikes the earth, splashing everywhere. In the midst of confusion, we notice this condition as it is. If we are present, we will not be conditioned by that movement. Dzogchen Semde calls it the state of *nepa*, calm. This is not to say that all movement disappears. To think that a state of calm is the state of contemplation is a mistake. Nobody is ever in a state where the mind is not functioning or energy is not manifesting. The quality of the mirror is that it can reflect, because if it does not, it is not a mirror. We have to discover and find ourselves in that condition. The movement will then no longer have the power to disturb us. If we are disturbed by movement or thoughts, everything becomes a burden. We cannot relax when distracted in this manner and even if we try, it is not true relaxation. That is why we should relax internally in the midst of the movement.

4.2.3.4.2 The Second Nyam
The second experience occurs when one is already in the state of *nepa*. In this state, certain characteristic experiences develop. We can utilize the example in the first experience: the water that has crashed down in the waterfall becomes a stream which makes some noise and has some movement but is not as violent as that of a waterfall. There is still movement but it is more coordinated and harmonized.

When one is present, at that moment one is no longer disturbed by the defect of sleepiness or agitation, but one who is not continuously present is still easily distracted. That is the example of the stream and the second kind of experience, *thobpai nyam*, or the experience of obtainment, as explained in the *Rigpai Khujug*. One finds oneself in the state of calm but staying relaxed in that state for too long or if a strong movement of thought occurs, one is immediately distracted. Nevertheless one has obtained the capacity to continue in presence.

4.2.3.4.3 The Third Nyam
The explanation of the *kompai nyam*, the experience of habit, refers to the process of repeating something many times and becoming ex-

tremely familiar with it, no longer having to observe or pay attention to what is happening. Things seem to happen spontaneously. Having this experience means being relaxed with presence whatever the relative condition of the body, voice, and mind. Even though causes may arise for the sleepy state or the agitated state, we can overcome them and continue in this relaxed presence, capable of contemplating in this state for a long time without distraction. The stream we used in the previous example has now become a flowing river still in movement. This is the experience of habit.

4.2.3.4.4 The Fourth Nyam

The next experience is the *tenpai nyam*, the experience of stability, meaning that even if one has many contacts with different secondary causes, one is able to remain in this presence undisturbed. In the Dzogchen Semde, after the state of *nepa* is the state of *miyowa*. In general many schools describe Shine and Lhagthong as varying ways in which body, voice, and mind manifest. In Sutra, for example, Lhagthong arises in us as we continue in the practice of Shine, whereas in the tradition linked to Tantrism, as in the Anuttaratantra, Lhagthong is the realization of what one applies in transformation, giving rise to the realization of clarity or development in our manifestation of energy as in the channels and chakras. Shine is taken to be emptiness and Lhagthong, energy or clarity. The union of the two is called *shilhag sungjug*, the union of Shine and Lhagthong, also known as *nangtong sungjug*, the union of vision and emptiness.

In the Dzogchen Semde, Lhagthong corresponds to the state of *miyowa*, no more movement, which however does not mean one is fixed and stationary. Movement refers to both the movement of the body and of energy which also represents our *prana*, vital energy, and above all, our karmic *prana*. Associated with the mind, this combination can create problems before the stage of *miyowa* is reached because this

CHAPTER FOUR *Long Commentary on the Rigpai Khujug*

energy does not leave a person in peace, but disturbs him. *Miyowa* does not mean that that energy has been cancelled, but rather that it can no longer be a cause of distress. Aspects of our body, voice, and mind which might have harassed us no longer have the power to do so. Now we are in the nature of the mirror, because whether the reflections are beautiful or ugly, they cannot disturb the nature of the mirror. That is one of the characteristic outcomes of integration.

A person following the Buddhist Sutra who starts to meditate tries to find internal peace and calm. For example, a practitioner hears the noise of a car nearby and feels that he cannot stay there to practice Shine because as soon as he enters the state of calm the car starts rumbling and he does not remain tranquil. After a while, he goes to live on a mountaintop. This is a typical course of action for one who strives only to stay in Shine, the state of calm. Beginners are disturbed and annoyed by thoughts and movement arising in their meditation, because they have not integrated with all the movements. They are not yet in this presence. They are still working mainly with experiences. That is why Sutra does not speak of *rigpa* which is related to the specific way of doing meditation and contemplation in Dzogchen.

We have five senses and the objects of the five senses. If I hear a sound, it is an object of one of my senses, and I consider that sound as pleasant, unpleasant, or neutral. If it is a sound like classical music which does not disrupt one, then I say it is pleasant. If a car makes a clamorous racket, then I say that it is disturbing. That means we still have the consideration of nice or unpleasant, like or dislike, and we have not integrated with the object. When we are in the state of the nature of the mirror, these concepts no longer exist. Whether a mirror reflects beauty or ugliness, there is no difference between them. Integration means this: presence, without creating the idea of subject and object.

In the process of integration, we first integrate with the mind, then with energy, and then with the material body. This is because we live in a karmic condition. Everything we see and touch is the result of our karma. To dissolve the karmic condition and integrate it into our true condition takes time. It is not sufficient to know that ice comes from water. Pouring a glass of water onto somebody's head will not hurt, but if you take the same amount of water turned to ice and throw it at somebody's head, you are not going to stop a hurtful blow by saying, "The origin of this ice is water." This is the result of karma. We may know the real meaning but it does not correspond to our actual condition. That is why we develop by integrating the mind, voice, and body in that order.

Someone in the state of *miyowa* and in the state of contemplation is first of all integrating with the mind. When one succeeds in integrating with energy, then phenomena known as miracles can happen. The *tenpai nyam*, or experience of stability is therefore the same as *miyowa*.

The river in the previous example finally becomes the ocean. All kinds of movements can be seen: above the ocean birds fly, on it boats sail, and in its depths are also sharks and other sea life, but however much they move, they cannot agitate the sea. Through our presence, we notice all the movements with our senses. Whatever the circumstances, whatever contacts our senses have with causes, there is no disturbance, only calm. This is called the experience of stability.

4.2.3.4.5 The Fifth Nyam

At the end is the *tharchinpai nyam*, the experience of accomplishment, which indicates to the practitioner that now he is in the state of integration. His presence is precise. An example is that of somebody going to sleep at night. At night, when we sleep, we do the night practice. We visualize a white A to continue this presence. The goal is to be in the presence of *chizhinwa*. Regardless of the practice one does, when one falls asleep, automatically presence arises. If one has become familiar with it and its presence during the day is stable, then as soon as one falls asleep and is in the dream state in which the mind begins to function, presence is activated. That is what we called *tharchin pai nyam*, the final experience of accomplishment. *Tharchin* means something is being accomplished. This experience is one that indicates that a person has accomplished the practice, referring to a person's ability to apply this state of contemplation in any circumstance and any situation, meaning that one is present in all circumstances, dead or alive. The moment one is in the *bardo* state, the manifestation of *sambhogakaya* is ready instantly. The practice called *chizhinwa* is this continuation of presence.

4.2.3.5 The Summary of the Practice

In general when we explain the way to continue in the state of contemplation, we relate it to our condition. Contemplation is related to emptiness, to sensation, or to clarity because the characteristic states of *nepa*, calm and *gyuwa*, movement are present. For example, if a thought arises and we do not follow it, we cannot say anything about where it came from, where it is now, and where it is going. The appearance is there, but if one observes this thought to find out where it is, it disappears. Nature itself is like this. The essence is empty means this. It is true not only of our thoughts, but also of our material body. For example, we may have a headache. If all we are aware of is how painful it feels, then it seems that we really have a headache. We are not pretending and do feel it, but if we observe this pain, where it is, what it is, we find nothing. If we look at it that way, perhaps we will feel less pain. This is because the essence is empty, so although it manifests, it is something we cannot find.

Nepa, calm, which is the characteristic of nature, means empty with nothing to confirm. The Buddhist Sutra speaks about absolute emptiness. When one searches mentally, one finds emptiness; and if one remains in that state of calm, it is called *nepa*. People who do Shine try to find themselves in this state of calm. Then there is *gyuva*, the characteristic of which is movement. When a thought arises, we look at it and find nothing. Emptiness is there, but thoughts continue to arise.

Of the four *tingedzin* or the Four Contemplations spoken of in Dzogchen Semde, the first is *nepa tingedzin*, the contemplation of calm, linked to Shine, the state of calm. Finding oneself in the state of calm is an experience, not contemplation. In Semde, the contemplation of calm is spoken of because the master indicates that when a practitioner is in the state of calm, this is an experience. It is up to the disciple to discover who is in this state of calm. There is a presence, and remaining in that presence is the discovery of the contemplation of *nepa*. *Nepa* is the same as *shunyata*, emptiness. Knowing that this emptiness is an experience, one stays in the presence of *rigpa* and that is contemplation.

Many people wonder whether the state of *shunyata* in the Buddhist Sutra is the same as the state of contemplation in Dzogchen. One cannot say either they are or they are not the same, because it depends on who is in this *shunyata*. If one is in the state of presence in the state of *shunyata*, then it is the same as contemplation. If one is using reason to arrive at emptiness and is only staying in the state of calm, that is not the same as contemplation.

The principle in Dzogchen is *rigpa*, the recognition of presence. *Rigpa* can be accompanied by various experiences, especially those of *nepa* and *gyuva*. Garab Dorje said in an important phrase, "Observe if thought or movement arises." To observe means being present. The arising of thoughts or movement means *gyuwa*. When observed, the movement of thoughts disappears. When the movement disappears one finds oneself in the state of calm. There is no difference. This means that when meditating, one must not search to obtain a state of calm, because calm is an experience, not contemplation. That is why Garab Dorje said, "There is no difference between the arising of movement and the state of calm." But if we look at the experience, no one can say that there is no difference. Whether it is calm, movement, or any of hundreds of experiences, the important thing to know is the difference between experience and presence. When we know what *rigpa* means, we ought to know how to integrate with all these aspects in our presence. Then at last we can discover what Garab Dorje meant in telling us that no difference exists between movement and the calm state.

4.3 The Fifth and Sixth Verses

ཟིན་པས་རྩོལ་བའི་ནད་སྤངས་ཏེ།
ལྷུན་གྱིས་གནས་པས་བཞག་པ་ཡིན།

Sinpa tsolwai ned pangte
Lhungyi nepe zhagpa yin

Since everything is complete in itself,
 abandoning the illness of effort,
One remains effortlessly present in
 the state of Contemplation.

The last two lines explain the fruit of our practice, and our attitude and behavior. Attitude is important in Dzogchen although not because of the existence of rules about what you should or should not do. Learning the Dzogchen teaching means becoming responsible for oneself. No one is going to tell you what to do. The teaching makes you understand that you must be responsible for yourself and this is an aspect of awareness. With the presence of awareness we can integrate our knowledge of contemplation into daily life. This is why attitude is important.

To integrate contemplation into attitude, first of all we must thoroughly understand what contemplation is. When we have accomplished that, we try to find ourselves in a state of presence all the time. The principle of *samaya*, Guruyoga, and so on is in that presence. That does not deny the value of doing other practices. The principle of Dzogchen is called *machöpa*, without correcting or conditioning, to continue as it is, but many people misunderstand this and instead of staying relaxed in that presence, they become lazy. They think that in order not to condition themselves, doing Dzogchen practice means doing nothing. A Dzogchen master teaches and transmits this state of relaxation, explaining how to remain in the state of presence and how not to charge yourself. He does not advise people to stay in a state of distraction, a danger if one misunderstands the teaching.

When Master Padmasambhava taught Dzogchen, he said that the way of seeing is to follow Dzogchen, but that behavior should follow the Vinaya or the Mahayana, not Dzogchen. Padmasambhava did not consider it wrong to be responsible for oneself but a matter of prudence not to confuse things. If one understands what the teaching is for, then one must remember the goal.

A disciple of Padmasambhava the great practitioner of Dzogchen and renowned scholar Nubchen Sangye Yeshe introduced the Anuyoga teachings to Tibet. He wrote a marvelous book that we still have today called *Samten Migdrön, The Light of the Eye of Contemplation*. One of its most detailed explanations is on Atiyoga or Dzogchen that at one point says many teachers have taught that the principle of *machöpa* does not lead to the state of contemplation which cannot be reached without rectifications. These teachers may claim to be teaching Dzogchen, but they are actually telling people to make many corrections. This is an error, like shooting an arrow without knowing what one is aiming at. You must not do things in that way if you are learning Dzogchen. You must know what the goal is. At the same time, you have to know what your own capacity is. If I am incapable of living with awareness and cannot be responsible for myself, then conditioning myself in some way or limiting myself a little is not such a bad thing: I cannot make it on my own, but I also know that this limitation is not the true final point. I am not confused but am just co-operating with myself.

Take drinking as an example. A drunkard who always drinks until he is half mad might know that it is not good for his health and his clarity of mind. He may have discovered that it is harmful to carry on in this way. That is called awareness but because he is an alcoholic and has this urge to drink, he cannot make this awareness function. In this case, although he is aware of it, he cannot overcome it. Thus he takes a vow from a master or commits himself by saying that he is not going to drink any more. He knows that the principle is not the taking of a vow or limiting himself, but that it is necessary for the moment and he does it with awareness. Using the body to control the mind or the mind to control the body, in one way or another he tries to overcome his alcohol addiction. For instance, the moment he picks up a bottle with his left hand, his right hand takes a stick and hits it. This is one way of doing things. It does not mean that you must not renounce certain things or follow rules. Of most importance is to be aware of circumstances, and our capacity in relation to them.

Dzogchen often talks about the capacity of the individual and says it is a teaching for people with superior capacity. A person with superior capacity is not enlightened or with limitless ability to do everything. Capacity is relative to the circumstances where it is needed. If we have awareness, but in practice this awareness is not functioning, we should know how to intervene in some way or, in other words, how to construct the capacity needed for the circumstances.

Although awareness is important, it is not as important as presence. Sometimes awareness means only a particular knowledge. For example, you may have an awareness of the consequences of a certain action. If I know that if I take poison I will die, this is called having an awareness of the consequence of taking poison, but if that awareness is not present in me at the necessary moment, it is just a fragment of knowledge. Many people have died taking poison although they knew it was poison, taking it because their attention was distracted due not only to confusing circumstances but also to passions such as anger.

Two persons are said to be in love. There is a time when it looks as if they cannot be separated. It seems that they are always embracing each other. When they eat, they even have to sit on the same chair. Blinded by passion, they do not know that what they are doing is false. If they sit on the same chair embracing each other when they are old, perhaps their love is real, but they are unlikely to be doing that because that falsification goes on for a first year or a first month or perhaps only for the first few weeks. Afterward, a little staleness sets in as the sensation begins to fade. It is no longer comfortable sitting on the same chair and it is an annoyance even if the two chairs are near each other. Sleeping together seems unpleasantly sweaty and even stroking each other is avoided because their hands feel rough to each other. That is how it usually develops. Then, like in films when people get angered, they grab a bottle of whisky and drink it down defiantly or if a bottle of poison is around, they drink that instead and think they are making a point. This is the other major distraction, distraction through passion, of which many kinds exist in life. Even though there is awareness, it does not work in those moments.

A Dzogchen practitioner has to have this presence in mind and try to be aware. He or she should know what the real condition is and should not falsify it. Relationships between people are an example of how practitioners should know what their condition really is. Some may wonder, "What has that to do with contemplation? It is not meditation." Actually it is really important. If two people understand and co-operate with each other, it can be an advantage for them. A lack of understanding and co-operation creates problems and can become a serious obstacle if the people involved are practitioners.

CHAPTER FOUR *Long Commentary on the Rigpai Khujug* 91

In life, it is natural for a man and a woman to become a couple. Since that is the natural way, we have to be aware of the situation. If two practitioners are together, they should not base their relationship on blind passion, because such a relationship is false and the consequences can be serious. Passions produce negative karma, so practitioners must be aware of them.

One does not have to renounce passion or refuse to recognize its value. Knowing the nature of passion, one can integrate that with practice. In Tantrism, passions are transformed into wisdom. Likewise in Dzogchen, if one knows how to be in the state of *chizhinwa*, this presence is linked to all experiences. All our sensations and our circumstances linked to the passions are experiences. It is not necessary to devalue the passions nor does it mean that a practitioner should become a block of stone. It is the opposite: a practitioner must experience all the manifestations of this energy, notice them, and integrate everything in contemplation. The point is not to be distracted by what is happening. In terms of attitude, the integration of contemplation into our life is based on this presence. That is why we try to be present in life as it is.

Sinpa means from the very beginning everything is fulfilled, accomplished. There is nothing to build or to do. There is no effort, because effort is linked with the mind. If one does not have that knowledge or that knowledge is not present, one must try to have it. Until one has that capacity, one must try in different ways to build it. In this case, one should not think that in Dzogchen effort and learning are all negated.

Everyone must do his or her best. Doing one's best means knowing oneself and one's own capacity. An important saying in Dzogchen is "Help yourself by collaborating with yourself." One can only do so by knowing one's own condition. If I lack a certain capacity, I should try to construct it. If I am confused, I should give myself space. If I am hungry, I should eat. If I am tired and tense, I must relax, rest, or sleep. All those considerations mean I recognize my condition. I am not trying to force myself. If I actually do something like striking my left hand with my right hand, I do that only with the understanding of the goal. In this way, we cultivate an attitude of responsibility toward ourselves, rather than accepting that someone else tells us what to do. Nor is it the same as thinking to refrain from doing something or that negative karma will be the outcome. In that case, it is only fear which stops one from acting. That point of view is called the way of renunciation and is only directed at overcoming negative causes, an outlook insufficient for Dzogchen where the nature of everything has to be understood.

Not only understanding the nature of the mind is meant here as the relative condition of body, voice, and mind is even more important. Whenever people hear cited the nature of the mind beyond concepts and so forth, they think, "How profound," but the real condition is more significant than talking about the nature of the mind. It is much better to know our own condition at which point it becomes meaningful to talk about the nature of the mind. Without understanding what the mind is, how can one really understand its nature? We have to discover the mind for ourselves. Linked to our physical energy and our physical body, the mind is linked to the body in the same way that the material body is linked to the material world. Because of this, we have many limits. If it is cold, we have to cover ourselves. If we are hungry, we have to eat. It is not enough to think that eating and not eating are the same or to say that in the nature of the mind, food does not exist. It does not apply because we have a material body which is linked to the material world. If something is big, it is not small. If it is white, it is not black. These are our limits. Since this is a limited material world we are living in, this is what we must concretely understand first. Following that, talking about the nature of the mirror can make sense because the aspects of body, voice, and mind are all limited like the reflections in the mirror. If we can understand the aspects of our existence, we have the possibility to understand its nature.

When we learn and apply practices in Tantrism, OM, A and HUM are used to represent the three states of Body, Voice, and Mind and are called the Three Vajras. In this case, the real condition and not the relative level of body, voice, and mind are referred to. This idea becomes meaningful if we know our relative condition. It is better to observe our existence and discover its condition. When we have discovered the limits and characteristics of our condition, we can really be aware of our existence. We can also be aware of the falsifying we create all the time, as well as of the real condition. This recognition is of the greatest importance for a Dzogchen practitioner, because even if one is doing a practice, without this awareness it is not real. Talking about integration will make no sense as it will just be the mind thinking that, "I want to integrate all this as everything seems to have the same nature." It does not correspond in practice.

Sinpa tsolwai ned pangte means it is important to find oneself beyond effort which is like an illness. At any given moment, finding oneself in that presence is the fruit, which is also contemplation. In the Dzogchen Semde, the final result is called *lhundrub*, which is neither a concept about realization nor the quality or description of a realized practitioner. What *lhundrub* does mean is that at all moments, our aspects of body, voice, and mind are integrated in contemplation. When we sleep, walk, eat, or perform any other activity, that moment is integrated in contemplation. That is how and what a practitioner has to develop. Doing a long retreat or going somewhere quiet to live for an extended period is not important. You can do those things if you feel like it or have the need, especially if you are incapable of integrating your practice in daily life, because you must do everything possible to achieve this integration. The most important factor is to have a precise experience of contemplation. For that, one must observe oneself.

Every time a master explains or transmits the teachings or when you read a text, you should examine yourself to see if you really understood. If you remain in doubt, not able to recognize if you are in the state of contemplation or not, many types of practice like the *semdzin* can make this certain. I have explained that many kinds of experience exist and that you must not confuse the experience with your felt presence in it. Try to gain some experiences from the practice. You do not have to do anything specific and can do any kind of practice. You will then understand what is meant by an experience. Having had all these experiences, one becomes more certain of what contemplation is.

We also often do practice together like Guruyoga, linking that with direct transmission. Every time we chant the *Song of the Vajra* together, the practice itself is the transmission. Moreover, the practice and transmission are linked with experiences. Everyone should do his or her best to discover the true experience of contemplation.

About attitude in Dzogchen, we say that at the beginning a practitioner has to have the attitude of a bee. A bee flies to all kinds of flowers, yellow, red, black, and blue. Smelling their scent, finding out if there is nectar to be had. This is the attitude without limitation a practitioner must be at the beginning, first of all, have no limitations with regard to meeting teachers, whether they are real masters or not. In general, an attitude of respect should be shown to a master because he teaches, as a mode of showing respect to the teaching. A master is not merely someone who sits in a special place and allows others to believe that they are his students. If I have to give teachings to two or three hundred people, surely I have to sit somewhere in order to explain and be heard. A master cannot talk to hundreds of people one by one, nor is it that he is performing like an actor in a theater and people watch. That is not the way of being for a master nor how the relationship between master and disciple should be.

Teaching can be given as a direct transmission. Also transmission can be oral. Oral transmission takes place when a master speaks to one or more others and the subject does not have to be a sacred text that the master reads from beginning to end. The topic of the discourse could be anything. For example, a master and a disciple might come across a dead mouse and the master says, "Smell it." If one understands, the stench itself can be the transmission. We do not have to look for a dead mouse nor do we have to smell an odor like that one. This is simply one example of the thousands of ways that exist. Through the experience of that odor, a master can enable a person to understand what is meant by the state of contemplation and how it is different from an experience. We smell a dead rat. We do not have to pretend. We really do smell it and we find that in no way is it a good odor. We know that it is unpleasant through our sense contact and our judgment, but if the person who is doing the smelling is in the state of presence, the reek of a dead rat or the fragrance of a French perfume is the same. If the teacher has been able to communicate that, then the smell of a dead rat is enough to open the path for that practitioner. Do not create limits in the master/disciple relationship. Everything has to be much looser. Do not think of the teaching as something sacred because it has to do with shelves of texts and books. The principle of the teaching is the understanding of knowledge.

Garab Dorje summed up the entire Dzogchen teaching in his *Three Statements* which form his famous testament.

The first statement is

Ngorang thogtu tred

ངོ་རང་ཐོག་ཏུ་འཕྲད།

or Direct Introduction. *Ngo* is a person's own condition as it is; the other words say to introduce his own condition directly to that person. It means that the master finds the way to introduce the state of understanding and enables a person to understand his own state. Thus the first statement is "Introduce the understanding of *chizhinwa*, the primordial state."

The second statement is

Thagchig thogtu ched

ཐག་གཅིག་ཐོག་ཏུ་གཅད།

or "Discover that understanding without any doubt." *Thagchig* means one state, the single presence. Even though thousands of experiences exist, that one state is the same. One does not remain in doubt about that understanding and therefore it is not a decision or a belief. If somebody believes or decides on something, it is false. One has to find this experience using different methods. Until we have direct experience of this understanding it is going to be false because a decision of the mind is not the real state of *rigpa*.

Dengdrol thogtu cha

གདེང་གྲོལ་ཐོག་ཏུ་འཆའ།

is the third statement, which means "Integrate that understanding into all circumstances in daily life and continue in this state of knowledge." Even though the Dzogchen teaching comprise hundreds of volumes of texts, Garab Dorje concluded and summarized them all in these three statements, possible because Dzogchen is an understanding not contained in words. In some way, since all the *tantras*, *lungs*, and hundreds of texts are relative, we have to absorb this understanding. Doing practice we gain a certain type of knowledge, and in that regard texts are useful and important because they explain different methods that enable us to have that experience and to develop the ultimate understanding.

The principal is knowledge, not what conventional thought finds important. More or less this is the essence of the Dzogchen teaching.

APPENDIX
A Brief Guide to the Methods and Traditions of Tibetan Buddhism

Different types of spiritual traditions can be found in Tibet which include the Nyingmapa, Kagyüdpa, Sakyapa, and Gelugpa, the four main Buddhist schools, as well as the ancient Bön teaching. Each of the four Buddhist traditions claims that it is the most perfect. If this were not their attitude, separate schools would not exist.

What is a school? Here it does not refer to one particular path or method of teaching, but to a global set of Buddhist teachings in which different paths exist. Some people who follow the Nyingmapa tradition, for example, say that Nyingmapa is Dzogchen. That is not the case. Nyingmapa also has Sutra, Mahayana, and Tantric teaching; it is a tradition with a global Buddhist teaching. Similarly, also Sutra and Tantra are found among the Gelugpas. As Tantrism is more developed in Tibet, all the Tibetan schools are exponents of Tantrism. However, if you follow a Tibetan Buddhist teaching or if you want to receive an important initiation such as the Kalachakra, you will be asked if you have taken refuge or not. If you say no, they will request you to take refuge first because although the refuge vow originates in the Hinayana teaching, it has been integrated into Tibetan Buddhism. Knowing the principles and the differences between the types of teaching and traditions is important because many people are confused regarding the varying titles, traditions, schools, and methods. Some even believe that differences exist among them as to the real meaning of the teaching. Since confusion is not the path to realization, we must know the characteristics of each type of teaching we follow.

1 Hinayana and Mahayana: the Path of Renunciation

Hinayana teaching and Mahayana teaching belong to the Sutra system and are called the path of renunciation. Characteristic of this path is to renounce the cause of negativity. Whoever is interested in the Buddhist teaching and reads Buddhist books usually is familiar with the Sutra, the teaching actually spoken by Buddha Shakyamuni in his manifestation as a human being. These explanations relate to our relative condition, so they work with and are intended to improve that condition. Sutra is, therefore, a simpler form of teaching designed to be understood by ordinary people. In it is the teaching of the Four Noble Truths found in both the Hinayana and the Mahayana traditions. Its real meaning is not so difficult, but when explained in an intellectual way it can become complicated. Although sometimes presented in three or four volumes in the form of analyses, Buddha taught it to ordinary people not as philosophy or a subject of study. Today it has become the main traditional study of all schools, and if you learn the Four Noble Truths in a monastery, it becomes really complex.

For example, many years ago I visited Switzerland and participated in meetings with young Tibetans. These young people felt that as Tibetans, they were Buddhist, even though they did not know what Buddhism is. They had invited a lama to give a teaching. For two hours this lama explained the principle of the Four Noble Truths in a convoluted and academic discourse. I am sure most of those young people did not understand anything, because although I had spent many years in college studying Buddhist philosophy, I could not understand what he was explaining. It only seemed that he had prepared extremely well:

analyses and words, quotations from which book, on which page, which line, and so forth. He really studied a great deal. If the Buddha had taught the Four Noble Truths that way, he would not have been able to communicate with peasants and ordinary people. If he had begun by talking about the nature of mind, only the intellectuals would have been able to understand, but anyway such people would never have agreed with him because of their own limited ideas. We are so used to confronting everything with our ideas that an intellectual explanation can only become a problem, not an understanding.

1.1 The Four Noble Truths

First Buddha taught the first noble truth of suffering. What does suffering mean? Suffering consists of whatever happens to our relative existence of body, voice, and mind. We have our first real direct knowledge of suffering through our material body, because whatever problem we may have at the level of mind or of voice energy will first manifest at the gross level, the body. It is easy for us to understand the meaning of suffering at this level. We do not have to be a learned scholar capable of deep analysis to understand this kind of affliction. We do not even need to have human consciousness to understand it; a dog or a cat also knows what suffering is because suffering is linked to our physical condition.

Since we do not enjoy suffering, why not try to seek a way out of it. In order to avoid suffering, some research into its cause is necessary. So Buddha taught the second noble truth of the cause of suffering. Using our reasoning power a little, we find a cause for our suffering, but it is not enough to discover only the cause. We need to bring about the cessation of that cause. For example, suppose an individual has a stomachache every day: he knows well that his stomach hurts and that he is suffering. If he is bothered sufficiently by this disturbance, he will want to discover the cause of it, or else he will continue to suffer. If he found that his ache is caused by bad food, he must do something about his discovery to stop his suffering.

Thus the Buddha began to teach the third noble truth of the cessation of suffering. Finally, Buddha taught the benefits of the cessation of suffering and the consequence of the noncessation of suffering. In this way he taught the law of cause and effect, the law of karma. If we need to bring about the cessation of suffering, what should we do? Many primary and secondary karmic causes exist, and ways of bringing about the cessation of these causes exist, but this is only working in a provisional way. If we want the complete and definitive cessation of suffering and the elimination of its causes, we must go beyond the relative condition entirely. That is why the concept of absolute and relative truth arose. The traditions of both Hinayana, the Small Vehicle, and Mahayana, the Great Vehicle, have the concept of the two truths, a main characteristic of teaching in the Sutra.

Buddha Shakyamuni manifested as a human being, a characteristic of the relative level of the teaching, to communicate the teaching to us human beings. Our way of understanding this teaching is to apply the rules of moral behavior. The basis of the approach in the Sutra is the practice of the way of renunciation: by avoiding negative behavior and cultivating positive virtues we can overcome our karma.

1.2 The Hinayana

The main concern of Hinayana teaching is to avoid creating problems for others by controlling our own behavior. The first thing done is to receive the refuge vow and keep certain rules. Hundreds of rules help us achieve this end. Buddha said, "Take the example of how you yourself feel and do not cause harm to others." If somebody is unkind to you, you notice it. Knowing what it is like to be disturbed, do not disturb others. The real sense of refuge is the acknowledgement of the path taught by the Buddha for realization. According to that path, you do certain actions and not others, controlling your behavior in that way.

When we take a Hinayana vow, we take it from now, this moment, until death. We do not take a vow from now until total realization. Why? Because a vow is linked to our present condition to be applied through our behavior which comes to an end when we die. Our body goes to the cemetery and we are finished with that particular vow. If until the moment of death we have maintained that vow purely, we have discharged a good action. No exceptions to the proper maintenance of such a vow are acceptable. We cannot vary it according to our own changing viewpoint. If a precise and genuine justification for handing a vow back manifests, no need to maintain it continues. Otherwise the vow remains binding from the moment we take it until the moment of our death. It is not correct to think that although we have taken the vow, we are free to act differently according to our intention.

Later, as the Hinayana system developed, not only was the refuge vow given to monks and nuns, but also the Upasaka vow to lay people to a vow that can be kept with only one rule, such as not killing, or two rules, such as with the addition of not stealing, and so on. Increasing levels can be chosen, until the complete vow of a fully ordained monk or nun is taken.

1.3 The Mahayana

The Mahayana teaching developed from the principle of intention. Rules were recognized as important for blocking negative causes, but were not considered a sufficient guide to living correctly. Instead, if we have good intentions, everything will have a good effect. The Tibetan Buddhist master Jigmed Linpa[1] said that if our intention is good, then the path and the fruit will be good; if our intention is bad, the path and the fruit will also be bad. Thus we must train in good intention.

Created later, in the Mahayana tradition today a vow is given called the bodhisattva vow, actually influenced by the Hinayana because originally no such thing as a bodhisattva vow was present. The principle of Mahayana is called *labpa* or training: the training of intelligence, the training of discipline which we need for co-ordinating our existence, and the training for our samadhi or contemplation. These three principles reveal that Mahayana is not only about self-control, but also about being ready to help others. The Hinayana principle is to renounce all disturbance and harm to others, while the Mahayana principle is to be ready to act to benefit others. That is the main difference.

Mahayana is the cultivation of *bodhichitta*, so that we check our intention in whatever we do because of its great importance in this particular teaching. Illustrating this principle of the Mahayana, a famous story of a mercantile chieftain who had taken the Hinayana vow not to kill relates how he led a group of traders to an island on an expedition to amass jewels. On the way back, one of them, an evil and powerful man, planned to kill the others in order to possess the entirety of the jewels. The head merchant discovered this man's intention and to stop the prospective assassin from accumulating infinite bad karma and to save everyone else's life, murdered him. He felt great guilt because he had broken his vow of not killing, as soon as he had returned to dry land, he went to Buddha Shakyamuni to confess. The Buddha said, "You have broken your vow, but you have not done anything negative. You did not kill with hatred or anger, but with compassion, to save that man from the consequences of his greed and to rescue the lives of others." This example given in the Mahayana Sutra illustrates the importance of intention. However, it certainly does not mean we ought to develop a good intention in order to kill people.

In Mahayana teaching, the two principles *mönpa* and *jugpa* mean respectively our intention to do something and the action we actually carry out. In *The Guide to a Bodhisattva's Way of Life*, the great master

Shantideva explains the difference is like planning to make a journey and actually packing a bag and leaving. The intention of doing practice to benefit others is *mönpa*, but a good thought is not enough. One has to enter into action in some way. For that reason when people start a practice they usually recite that they want to realize themselves for the benefit of all beings and are not trying to arrive at realization only for their personal benefit. Using these words becomes a mental training and what is meant by *bodhicitta*. Whether one uses words or not, the important point is to have the right intention.

Generally people think that Mahayana is more important than Hinayana because Mahayana means the great vehicle and Hinayana the lesser vehicle. This is a wrong idea. At the beginning, the Buddha presented his teaching in terms of suffering at a low level so that common people could understand and apply it, calling it *hina* or lesser for that reason. *Maha* or greater means that one is not limited and has the capacity to integrate more and to go beyond the norms of existence if one knows benefit can be gained for others. Both are from the Sutra, the oral teaching of Buddha Shakyamuni. The teachings which Buddha Shakyamuni gave on this earth to Indian people constitute Hinayana. Buddha, teaching at the Mahayana level and without transforming, contact other dimensions and talk with beings of higher capacity such as *nagas* and *devas*.

People who are capable of going further and applying Tantrism have more capacity and an understanding of energy, because our existence also encompasses energy and mind. Those who have a knowledge of the function of energy can discover the value of Tantric teaching. If we are ignorant of it or have no capacity to understand it, the Sutra method is more important for us. It depends on the ability of the individual. We should not judge, saying that one is more important than the other. Every teaching has perfect qualities, and we cannot classify it as good or bad. We can only say something about the capacity of persons who follow a certain teaching and the kind which suits best what kind of individual.

Since Sutra has always been the pillar of Buddhist teaching, if you want to present Buddhism, you talk about Sutra. That is why when Tantrism is taught it is often said that refuge and *bodhichitta* must not be lacking. By so doing we are incorporating the principles of Hinayana and Mahayana into the practice. These days some important lamas and teachers tend to talk about the two truths even when they give a Tantric teaching. This is really Sutra and not Tantra because the two truths are not mentioned in Tantrism. In Sutra, and in the Mahayana Sutra particularly, the principle of *shunyata* or void is presented. The *Prajnaparamita* or Heart Sutra is recited by practitioners of many Buddhist traditions, including Zen. This expounds the voidness of the self-nature of our body, our senses, and of all the phenomena of our relative condition, thus bringing us into the state of emptiness. Finding ourselves in this state we are said to be in the state of absolute truth, the state of meditation. For Tantra, however, voidness is merely the starting point.

Many masters when they discuss Tantra speak about voidness and compassion. As Nagarjuna said, "If there is the void without compassion, then that void is of no value." The same is explained in the *Mahamudra* of Saraha. However, here compassion does not just mean working with our intention, as we understand at the level of Mahayana Sutra. What is named compassion in Sutra is called energy in Tantra into which we enter and utilize.

2 Tantra: the Path of Transformation

We have our three levels of existence: body, voice, and mind. Buddha Shakyamuni manifested as a human being to teach Sutra which is mainly linked to the dimension of the body and therefore the accompanying vows, and so on. Linked to the dimension of voice is Tantrism which works with energy, voice being connected to one's breathing and thus to *prana* energy. Voice also means sound through which mantras are heard, and a mantra in turn is formed of syllables. That is why Tantrism is also called the Mantrayana. The syllables that we recite in Tantrism are symbols of forms of energy, not about repeating random words. It is important to understand the principle of Tantric transmission and how the principle of manifestation is related to it, otherwise Tantrism cannot be understood.

2.1 *The Source and Transmission of Tantra*

Those people who are conditioned by Sutra tend to say that Tantra was also taught by Buddha Shakyamuni. They usually say things like, "Buddha Shakyamuni transformed himself in order to give this teaching," also saying that one year before his *parinirvana* Buddha Shakyamuni manifested as Kalachakra. You can think of it that way if you want. We live within the limits of time and therefore have the idea that a manifestation must have actually taken place, but we must not think of Buddha Shakyamuni as an actor on a stage who appears in the theater one day as a monk and another in the *yabyum* form of male and female union. The original Tantric transmission does not involve talking and listening. Tantra is called the teaching of the *sambhogakaya* and a *sambhogakaya* manifestation like Kalachakra is beyond the consideration of time. The *samboghakaya* is the dimension of clarity and energy, a dimension which manifests its inherent qualities. If we stand in front of a mirror, we see our own reflection in it because although the mirror itself has no form, it has the potentiality to reflect infinite images. Similarly the *samboghakaya* has infinite potentiality to manifest which is why hundreds of forms of deities can be presented at the *sambhogakaya* level.

Sambhogakaya manifestations appeared first to those individuals who had sufficient capacity to receive such a transmission. For example the Kalachakra manifestation of Buddha Shakyamuni did not take place in front of average Indian people who were there by chance. Instead, individuals known as *rigdzin* with the capacity to receive the transmission of Buddha Shakyamuni were those in contact with the manifestation of Kalachakra.

In the Anuyoga history of the Nyingmapa school, different types of *rigdzin* such as *deva rigdzins, naga rigdzins,* and *rigdzins* of other dimensions have appeared. Why does one have to be a *rigdzin* to receive the transmission of this kind of teaching? The reason is this. The life history of Guru Padmasambhava tells us he did not have an ordinary death like human beings, but manifested the body of light through a practice known as the Great Transference. Manifesting the body of light means that the material body enters into its essential nature as light. The essence of our energy means the essence of the elements appears as colors. We consider that Guru Padmasambhava manifested in this way, although we cannot see him and his dimension because we have too many karmic traces. A *rigdzin* who has higher capacity can see Guru Padmasambhava and can receive transmission through various types of transformations. The transformation manifested and transmitted comes about according to the conditions that exist at the moment of the event. For example, the form of the *heruka* Hayagriva has a horse's head. This is because the class of beings whose form we recognize as having the head of a horse received the manifestation first. Similarly, the manifestation of the *dakini* Simhamuka has a lion face because we find it a possible way to describe her. If we want to approach Tantrism, we have to have a wider and more open view.

People generally have limited vision. When information is heard about other beings, they wonder if they can accept that. Knowing only human beings and animals, they do not believe that *nagas, devas,* and all sorts of different beings exist. It is not so difficult to understand, even logically. Today, scientifically speaking, we know the universe has many solar systems and galaxies. We cannot say that no other types of beings inhabit other solar systems and planets. Some say that since these beings cannot be seen, they do not exist, but we cannot see beyond a wall or places a long distance away nor what happened in the past either, although we believe it occurred. Logically speaking, we cannot with certainty state that such beings do not exist. Some animals or insects which we can see are not able to see us. Similarly, since we are also a sort of animal, there can be beings who can see us but we cannot see them. If we are aware of such conditions, we can benefit. Otherwise, we can have many problems.

Generally speaking, followers of Hinayana say that Hinayana is the real Buddhist teaching. They do not recognize other forms of teaching, saying that they are not certain whether Mahayana and Tantra are really the teachings of the Buddha. To dispute in this way is unnecessary. It is true that Buddha taught Hinayana as a teaching transmitted physically from one person to another, but many other types of knowledge have been introduced from other dimensions for our benefit in the human dimension as Mahayana, Tantra, and Dzogchen teachings. For example, the *Prajnaparamita* was taught by Buddha to the *nagas*, and later Nagarjuna introduced it from the *naga* realm to human beings.

It is important to know also that in our relative condition we can easily be afflicted by provocations from different kinds of beings. Since we cannot see them, we can instigate many problems by disturbing them, who in response can cause us serious harm. We then pay for our ignorance.

Although modern Bönpo often ignores its own ancient knowledge and often associates itself with Buddhist schools of thought, in the Bönpo tradition is much is to be learned about different types of beings. Researching into Bönpo traditions in villages where the inhabitants still do ancient rituals, one can find an understanding of the past even though the practitioners may not be able to explain a great deal. The

Bön have deep knowledge in this area and in the nature of energy, both of the individual and the individual's dimension, as well as the energy that links a person with other beings, how one can receive provocations, and how to overcome or pacify such provocations. That is the Bönpo specialty. Not only can we find such explanations in Bönpo books, we can also find hundreds of such books in Tibetan Buddhist teachings. This is because Guru Padmasambhava introduced Bönpo teachings of this type into Buddhism and transformed them with Buddhist principles. In the Nyingmapa tradition, in the last two or three of the eight series called *Jigten Chötöd* of the *Desheg Kagyed* or *The Eight Series of Tantras*, most of which are related to Anuyoga, are originally from the Bönpo tradition and system. Guru Padmasambhava also manifested in a wrathful form and created these teachings for the Tibetans. These are important books.

Because Tibet was originally the land of the Bönpos in ancient times, Tantrism is more diffused in Tibet. Before inviting Guru Padmasambhava to Tibet, the Tibetan king invited Shantarakshita, the most well-known pandit in India at that time, to Tibet to spread Buddhism. However, Shantarakshita did not succeed because of strong Bönpo resistance. Later, Guru Padmasambhava was invited whose teaching based on Tantrism is much concerned with explanations of energy. Ancient Tibetan knowledge was also deeply related to the functioning of energy. Even though the explanations of energy in Buddhism and Bön are slightly different, the principle is the same. That is why Tibetans integrated Buddhist Tantric teaching more easily than Sutra.

2.2 Divisions of Tantra

Tantra in three of the Tibetan Buddhist Tantric traditions is divided into lower and higher while in the Nyingmapa tradition, these divisions are called outer and inner. Lower Tantra is mainly the path of purification and higher Tantra, the path of transformation. Tantra means the continuation of energy. This recognition of the value of energy in an individual's existence is never mentioned in Sutra. In Sutra, the three passions of ignorance, attachment, and anger are called the three poisons and are considered negative. Because of them much negative karma is produced, and as a result one continues in infinite samsara. These three passions, the cause of this infinite samsara, are to be renounced as valueless according to Sutra. However, in Tantrism, although they are passions, their nature is energy which has its good and bad aspects. As the root of both is the same, to renounce that energy is mistaken because utilizing it to transform the passions, one benefits. The knowledge of Tantrism is the recognition of this energy.

The important lower Tantras are the Kriyatantra and the Yogatantra. In Kriyatantra, the most frequently practiced method is that of Tara or Avalokiteshvara after one receives the appropriate initiation and empowerment, which means working with energy as we prepare to gain the wisdom of that deity.

In general, enlightened beings have infinite commitments to all sentient beings. Everyday practicing *bodhichitta*, we create the commitment and promise to benefit all sentient beings. Enlightened beings went through that same process and therefore have accumulated infinite commitments, but we do not know if we have any relationship with them. If we had some contact with them when they were on their path as bodhisattvas, then we have a connection. In this case, we are the first to receive the transmission and can obtain enlightenment through the path of these realized beings. Otherwise, receiving an initiation and applying the related method is a way of creating that possibility.

When we receive an initiation, we also have a certain commitment. In Tantrism we must have a painting or statue of the deity, considered as the support of the deity and invite that deity to be present in the painting or statue. We present the deity with lamps, flowers, incense, and so forth, also making many imaginary offerings, thus accumulating merits. We pray that we may receive wisdom. Doing this type of practice in a lengthy way is a preparation for receiving wisdom.

Receiving the wisdom of Tara or Avalokiteshvara does not mean we will be enlightened immediately. Active preparation for receiving wisdom develops our clarity so that we know what the path is and how to develop our knowledge. It is not only praying but has to do with our condition, maybe enabling us to take a more important path such as that of Yogatantra. In Yogatantra, although similar to Kriyatantra, we unify ourselves with the deity, such as Tara. Also we transform into that deity and at the conclusion, at the unification stage, we become realized. Lower Tantra has the name Tantra because at the end you realize the wisdom of the deity which you have visualized as the model for your realization. Yogatantra, much diffused in Tibet, is the official Tantra teaching because it is similar to ordinary Sutra. You make offerings of nice things and you follow rules, so it combines easily with Sutra.

2.3 Higher Tantra

Anuttaratantra teaching is different, involving the transformation of passions into wisdom which is why limits are broken. If you normally strictly control your body, voice, and mind, when you transform you discover that such control is not the principle and so your behavior goes beyond limits. That is why many stories recount Indian *mahasiddhas* doing apparently strange things.

In Tantrism, many symbols can be found for breaking and integrating. We have the three passions which we transform in three methods. Anger is transformed into wrathful manifestations such as Simhamuka; ignorance is transformed into peaceful manifestations such as Vairochana; and attachment is transformed into joyful manifestations such as Hevajra or Chakrasamvara. These are the three root passions and examples of their wisdom aspects. If we visualize a wrathful manifestation, all circumstances are presented in wrathful form. The offering is no longer that of flowers or incense, but of an opposite sort like blood and flesh which is why Anuttaratantra is not easily combined with Sutra. Ordinary people cannot understand: on the one hand we must behave like a monk, and on the other we visualize male and female bodies in sexual union. The Sutra says that you should not drink even a drop of alcohol, but in the cycle of offerings of a Ganachakra or Ganapuja in the Anuttaratantra, we use meat and wine. The Tibetan kings who knew that Anuttaratantra was the most important teaching but found it inappropriate for the ordinary people who could not understand and would have found it provocative, applied and followed it in secret. Publically they declared Yogatantra the official teaching. Teachers taught Anuttaratantra to disciples only in secret, also applying it personally.

Later, Tibetan masters diffused the knowledge of Anuttaratantra by disguising it in the form of Yogatantra and transforming the way it was presented. After that, many rituals and ceremonies and objects developed for the transmission of Anuttaratantra. Before that, if a teacher wanted to give an initiation and transmit its knowledge, only a fragment of the drawing of a mandala or a statue was used, just to give the disciple an idea of how to manifest the form and enter into that dimension, not like Yogatantra where homage is paid to a statue on the altar in order to receive wisdom. Later, all monasteries became full of Anuttaratantra statues and mandalas. For example, the walls of a huge hall in Shalung Monastery in Tibet are covered in mandala representations intended as a form of art. Such paintings are used no longer only for giving an idea in a transmission.

Today it is extremely difficult to perform the Kalachakra initiation. A master like the Dalai Lama giving this initiation must prepare mandalas and different objects for many days. If you are not a rich man, you cannot do it. If someone asked me to give the Kalachakra initiation, it would be impossible, not because I have not had that initiation myself or I do not know how to give it, but because I do not have the objects. The system that has been presented in the Tibetan tradition has to be followed. That I could not do.

Originally, things were very different. Indian *mahasiddhas* went to Oddiyana to receive Anuttaratantra teachings such as Kalachakra or Hevajra so that later they could introduce these teachings in India. Arriving in Oddiyana, they would find the master sitting under a tree or in a cave, and they would ask him to give them his most important teaching. The master would probably say something like, "Alright, after three days let us meet at such a place in a cave at midnight," so at midnight the master transmitted Kalachakra or Hevajra. Many histories of the *mahasiddhas* describe it that way. This means that to have many objects is not necessary. Drawings of Dzogchen or Tantric masters often show a box called a *samatog* in which they kept objects for practice and for giving transmission. If you requested an Anuttaratantra teaching then, the teacher would have taken a small drawing of a mandala and something else out of the *samatog*, performed the initiation, and then it was over. It was nothing like these days. Over the centuries, each master added a little in the initiation process, with the result that now it is truly complicated.

Transmission in Tantra is a kind of introduction to how that transmission was received at the beginning. We already know that only highly realized beings are able to perceive a transmission through the manifestation of light. Later this transmission was introduced to students orally by a teacher who gives examples of mandalas with images, and so forth: this is known as initiation. A person enters into that knowledge and applies that method. At the end, the realization is called Mahamudra.

In the four main schools, the final goal of the path of transformation is Mahamudra. Many types of Mahamudra teaching are given these days. Particularly in the Kagyüdpa, the famous teacher Gampopa presented Mahamudra in a way which integrated Sutra and Tantra. It is important to understand that Mahamudra involves transformation into deities and that just integrating the state of transformation in the state of clarity is Mahamudra. If you do not understand this point, you cannot appreciate the importance of transformation, and you can also make other mistakes. Many Western translators translate the term Mahamudra as great seal which is totally wrong. Generally, seal refers to a means to prevent something from being known. Here, mudra has nothing to do with seal, but means symbol in the way we also refer to ritual hand gestures as mudras. A mudra has the function of communication. A manifestation of an enlightened being is like a reflection in a mirror. If a dog appears in the mirror, it means that a dog is in front of the mirror. The image in the mirror is a symbol of potentiality, not the potentiality itself. Through that symbol you can understand what the potentiality is. In Tantrism, everything is none other than a symbol. You recite mantras and visualize deities and mandalas: everything is a symbol for realizing the real potentiality. Mahamudra means your existence of body, voice, and mind is totally in that clarity.

If you transform into, say, Kalachakra, associated with it is its dimension of transformation called the mandala. If you are present in it and are no longer constructing anything, in that instant you are in Mahamudra. Until you have that presence, you build things one by one, a process called *kyerim*, the development stage, followed by *dzogrim*, the completion stage, in which everything is integrated in this manifestation with your channels, chakras, and energy points. Finally you enter that clarity. Without this principle, you are missing the important point in Tantrism. You may even think that the deity and initiation are like a passport for arriving at Mahamudra as if it were another teaching.

The practice of Tantrism works with movement which is why we visualize as well as sing, chant, and do sacred dances, integrating everything in the state of contemplation. These movements are more important than remaining in silence. It is easier to enter into the state of contemplation in silence, but both silence and movement are our natural condition. Knowing how to use both modes in our practice, we can realize our practice more quickly. That is why we say Tantra teachings lead one to realization more swiftly than those of Sutra.

2.4 Divisions of Higher Tantra

In the Nyingmapa school, the higher Tantra is divided into Mahayoga, Anuyoga, and Atiyoga. The first two are the path of transformation and Atiyoga, the last, is the path of self-liberation. The transformation practice has two distinct types of visualization: the gradual and the nongradual methods. Gradual transformation belongs to Mahayoga, and nongradual to Anuyoga. Mahayoga in the Nyingmapa tradition corresponds to Anuttaratantra in other schools. In Anuttaratantra, great emphasis is given to the careful developing of visualization and the importance of clear visualization of the forms and colors of the transformation. The potentiality is called the seed syllable because the result of the potential cannot be seen yet, just as a flower seed will only become a flower if it is planted in the earth and given water and sunshine. When the plant blooms, the color, form, and fragrance of the flower emerge, just as in the practice, you slowly develop the manifestation from the seed syllable. You have to mentally build the details of the visualization one by one, starting from, for example, the first hand on the right which holds a particular ritual implement, then the second hand which holds a different object, and so on. *Kyerim* is concluded when you have constructed the entire mandala perfectly. When this visualization is complete, you work with integrating it through your energy, channels, and chakras. The entire manifestation will then become really alive. In the clarity of this presence, it is called the Mahamudra. This is gradual transformation.

In Anuttaratantra, no mention is made of a word like gradual. In Anuyoga, Anuttaratantra or Mahayoga is described as gradual because Anuyoga uses a nongradual method. From the beginning, the explanation of our real nature given in Anuyoga is presented in the same way as in the Dzogchen teaching. We do not mention a seed of potentiality. Instead we speak of our state of Dzogchen, the self-perfected state that has nothing to develop or change. Our real nature is as it is, pure from the beginning. Since it is self-perfected from the start, nothing is to be created. We say that realization results when our nature manifests, which does not mean our real nature has changed or developed because there is nothing to perfect.

How does this self-perfected state manifest in Tantra? It manifests through transformation, that is, Anuyoga. Anu means superior which means although Tantrism and the path of transformation are generally important, this particular method is the most essential and highest within Tantrism itself. When we apply the Anuyoga system, we do not need to construct things one by one through transformation. Having the knowledge of our real condition as it is is considered to be most important in Anuyoga. Manifesting or transforming into the form of a deity means being how it is, not that we are changing, building, or assembling. Not possessing the state of knowledge because we are conditioned by dualism, in order to find ourselves in that true condition again, we learn from the master who teaches us and enables us to enter into that state of knowledge which is our own condition. This is called transmission and it is of great importance to receive the transmission and apply it to enter that state instantly.

If I transform into Kalachakra in the Anuyoga style, for example, having that knowledge from the beginning, instantly I am in that vision, that presence, and that vibration. We enter into that presence directly instead of constructing something. Just that is sufficient in Anuyoga; that is its great difference from Anuttaratantra. In the transformation practice of Anuyoga, it is not so important to visualize things precisely and clearly. If you cannot see forms or colors perfectly, it does not matter. All you need is an idea. You get the idea in the transmission, and you get the feeling for it and apply it later. If you do not feel or have that vibration, even if you see the colors precisely, it is not important in Anuyoga. In Anuyoga, the state of realization is called Dzogchen, not Mahamudra.

Officially, no division into three yogas in the higher Tantra exists which also includes practitioners of Dzogchen-Atiyoga. Only Anuttaratantra is recognized as having three divisions, father Tantra, mother Tantra, and neutral Tantra, according to the emphasis in the transformation practice. The Sakyapas, for example, recognize all three types of Tantra, whereas the founder of the Gelugpa Tsongkapa (1357-1419) asserted that only father Tantra and mother Tantra exist, and there is no neutral Tantra. The real meaning of such division is that if the method presented in the Tantra emphasizes visualization, that is, the development stage, it is considered a father Tantra; if the method puts more emphasis on working with channels and chakras, that is, the completion stage, it is considered a mother Tantra. An example of father Tantra is the Guhyasamaja, an example of mother Tantra is Chakrasamvara. In some traditions such as that of the Sakyapas, Kalachakra and Hevajra are classified as neutral Tantras because the emphasis on the two stages of transformation practice is quite balanced.

Since only the Nyingmapa school has the gradual and the non-gradual method of transformation as well as Atiyoga, many Nyingmapa masters analyze the three yogas – Maha, Anu, and Ati – in such a way as to correspond to the father, mother, and neutral Tantra types, in a sort of amiable gesture to the other Tibetan Buddhist traditions. That analysis does not in fact correspond at all. All three types of Tantra are gradual transformation methods and both the gradual and nongradual transformation practices work with channels and chakras. Each Tantra is a path in itself at this level, so the comparison of the three yogas with the three types of Tantra has little meaning.

The Tibetan Book of the Dead describes manifestation as occurring in terms of sound, rays, and lights. These are the principles of manifestation. Rays and lights are linked to the dimension of sound and energy. The transformation is the form which arises with rays and light. That instantaneous manifestation is then brought into the oral tradition and an intellectual explanation is given of various symbols and so forth and of the method which we should practice to carry ourselves into that state. The manifestation itself is the way to enter into that dimension. In Tantra, the method that brings us into the dimension of the original manifestation is the path of transformation. The real meaning of the word Tantra refers to our own condition which is the continuation of energy, so Tantra is the method by which we find ourselves in that condition.

3 Dzogchen, the Path of Self-Liberation

The third inner Tantra according to the Nyingmapa tradition of Tibetan Buddhism is Atiyoga, also known as Dzogchen. However, Dzogchen is not the final goal of Anuyoga, the path of nongradual transformation. Atiyoga is not a Tantric path; it is the path of self-liberation.

Ati is a word in the Oddiyana language which means primordial state. Its method is about how to discover that state which is also called *Thigle Chenpo*, Total Thigle. A *thigle* is a sphere of light, the symbol of potentiality, *chenpo* is total, so total *thigle* means everything is perfected in that potentiality. It has no corners, signifying the absence of limitations. In some ancient Dzogchen texts, *changchub*, or *bodhicitta* is used for Dzogchen, but do not understand *bodhicitta* in the same way as in the Sutra systems. Mahayana teaching speaks of absolute and relative *bodhicitta*. Absolute *bodhicitta* is the state of emptiness, but having a knowledge of emptiness and the state of Dzogchen are not always the same. These two words, *chang* meaning purified, without any negativity and *chub* meaning perfected, represent *kadag* and *lhundrub* in the Dzogchen teaching.

Atiyoga is the path of self-liberation, but many teachers teach it in a Tantric way because Tantrism is the most important teaching presented in Tibetan Buddhism, and thus people tend to consider Dzogchen in terms of the path of transformation. An important Nyingmapa scholar Ju Mipham wrote a book in which he insisted that in Dzogchen there is *kyerim* and *dzogrim*, the development stage and the completion stage. Why? Because if one had said that these two stages are not present, the other schools, totally influenced by the path of transformation, would have said that Dzogchen was not a valid path. In view of the prevailing attitude of the other schools, some Nyingma scholars found it distinctly uncomfortable to maintain the existence of a perfectly valid path which had nothing to do with transformation practice. The other schools also found it hard to accept Dzogchen as a wholly self-sufficient path in its own right.

The result of trying to maintain a smooth relationship with other schools is that many teachers later integrated Dzogchen into Tantric practices. Today when you receive a Dzogchen Upadesha teaching, first of all you receive a form of initiation considered highly important. You can transmit the knowledge of Dzogchen through initiation and it is a correct way, but it does not accord with the Dzogchen characteristic of discovering ourselves.

Dzogchen is called the teaching of the mind of Samantabhadra which signifies that Dzogchen teaching is given in direct relation to our mind and not to our body or our voice energy. We use the mind to enter into the state of knowledge. The principle of Dzogchen is not meditation but the state of knowledge. Many practices in Dzogchen enable us to enter, develop, and ultimately realize this state of knowledge. We integrate this state into all our life's activities at the level of our mind.

Dzogchen can be transmitted orally, where the teaching is explained in an intellectual way; symbolically, using forms and ceremonies such as initiation; or directly, without using words or symbols. This is because we have a body, voice, and mind, the three aspects of our existence. Just as we have three different paths, the path of renunciation, the path of transformation, and the path of self-liberation, Dzogchen has these three different types of transmission, each corresponding to an aspect of our existence. Oral transmission can very well be done intellectually, but it is not necessarily the most important way of transmission. A teacher who communicates with a person who has studied Buddhist philosophy for many years will find it easy to explain using that system even though this method will not work for everyone. For example, one of the root texts in Dzogchen was written by Manjushrimitra who was a great scholar. For others, perhaps initiation is more important, because they are so used to ceremony. Much depends on individual circumstance.

Dzogchen is generally presented in three series, called Semde, Longde and Upadesha, which correspond to the three ways of transmission. These three series, not to be seen as three schools or traditions, are presented in this way in order to relate to the different capacities of individuals to understand and to enter into the state of knowledge.[8] The capacities of individuals are obviously not equal; some in order to find themselves in the state of knowledge needing to work more through the control of their body and others through the control of their mind. This experience may arise through the master's direct introduction, but even so, still something remains to be worked on and developed.

Dzogchen was principally taught by Master Garab Dorje. His last testament of three statements is a resume of the entire Dzogchen teaching. The three series of Semde, Longde, and Upadesha are the three ways of practicing according to Garab Dorje's three statements. His first statement is direct introduction, meaning we enter directly into the state of knowledge. In Semde, the first series of Dzogchen teaching, we work with the four *naljors* or yogas to find ourselves in the presence of the state of knowledge. This series not only deals with the introduction of knowledge, but has hundreds of methods available for arriving at total realization. The emphasis is on gaining a direct experience of the primordial state of the individual.

The second series of Dzogchen teaching, the Longde, works with the second statement of Garab Dorje, not remaining in doubt. That does not mean arriving at a decision intellectually where the choice would be arbitrary and false. When we have a truly authentic experience, nothing is false, nothing is to be decided. In Longde, we work with the four *Das* or symbols to find ourselves concretely in a live experience of the state without a shadow of doubt, although Longde also has a method of direct introduction to the state and of continuation in it.

The third series of Dzogchen teaching, the Upadesha, works mainly with the third statement of Garab Dorje: continuing in the state, the state about which we have no doubt. The Upadesha emphasizes direct introduction less and the continuation in the state of contemplation more. Again, all methods relating to Garab Dorje's three statements are contained in the Dzogchen Upadesha in which series the Tregchöd and Thögal methods are explained. The Tregchöd instructs us how to continue with the Four Chogzhags, which means remaining relaxed in our present condition, just as it is, without changing anything. When a practitioner's Tregchöd is stable, the Thögal method is employed for bringing about the dissolution of karmic vision more rapidly. Our reason for following the teaching is to realize ourselves. If we achieve total realization, we can truly speak of benefiting others. It is for this reason also that we are interested in realization.

Some people who practice Sutra are concerned about the consequences if they practice Tantra. Others wonder that if they have had a master in another tradition, what will occur if they follow the Dzogchen teaching. In reality, we are not interested in realizing a school or a tradition or a teaching. Investigation at the level of schools and traditions does not influence the process of self-realization a great deal. The reason we want to know the differences is so that we are not confused. Fixing on them is not the point. Instead, we should do our best to develop awareness and knowledge of the teachings and integrate everything.

ABOUT THE AUTHOR

Born in1938 in a family of great Dzogchen practitioners, Chögyal Namkhai Norbu is one of the foremost living masters of Dzogchen. He belongs to the last generation of Tibetans to have been fully educated in Tibet.

Recognized as a reincarnation of the eminent Dzogchen master Adzom Drugpa (1842-1924), he studied with renowned masters of various Tibetan Buddhist traditions at important colleges, demonstrating exceptional capacity to learn and receiving degrees in both philosophy and letters and traditional medicine. Among his teachers were his maternal uncle, Khyentse Chökyi Wangchug, and his paternal uncle Ugyen Tendzin, who realized the rainbow body, the foremost achievement for a Dzogchen practitioner.

After being invited to Italy in the 1960s by Professor Giuseppe Tucci (1894–1984), a leading scholar in Asian studies, to work at the Italian Institute for the Middle and Extreme Orient, he began to give instructions to a small group of students on Yantra Yoga, an ancient form of Tibetan Yoga combining movement, breathing, and visualization. He then started to give Dzogchen teachings to an ever-growing following of Western students forming the core of what has grown into the International Dzogchen Community, a worldwide association of people who share an interest in the knowledge and practice of this ancient spiritual path.

Chögyal Namkhai Norbu travels throughout the world, giving teachings and speaking at international conferences. A prolific author of books on Dzogchen, Yantra Yoga, and Tibetan history and culture, he founded ASIA and the Shang Shung Institute (now called the Ati Foundation), two nonprofit organizations dedicated to supporting the Tibetan people and preserving Tibetan culture.

With his simple and communicative style, he is able to reach all kinds of audiences, and doesn't give too much importance to his many titles. When sometimes asked about his previous incarnations, he is fond of saying: "I am just Namkhai Norbu. This for me is more concrete, more important."

GLOSSARY
of Tibetan Terms[1]

AMDO (*a mdo*) — one of the three traditional regions of Tibet (the other two being Ü-Tsang and Kham)
BARDO (*bar do*) — intermediate state
BÖN (*bon*) — pre-Buddhist religious tradition of Tibet
BÖNPO (*bon po*) — a practitioner of Bön
CHA (*cha*) — part
CHAMPA (*byams pa*) — love, compassion
CHANGCHUB SEM (*byang chub sems*) — bodhichitta
CHASHE (*cha shas*) — a single thing, partial
CHATSOL DRALWA (*bya rtsol bral ba*) — without effort
CHAWÖN (*bya 'on*) — an illness related to low blood pressure
CHEN (*chen*) — great, total
CHIGPU (*gcig pu*) — unique taste
CHIGTHOG (*gcig thog*) — one state
CHINGWA (*bying ba*) — drowsiness, sleepiness
CHIZHINWA (*ji bzhin ba*) — as it is
CHÖ (*chos*) — the Teaching, the Dharma
CHÖD (*gcod*) — the practice of cutting off one's attachment to ego by offering one's body

---

1 The definitions in these glossaries are mainly drawn from the Oral Commentary to the Rigpai Khujug, so they are not meant to be complete, but refer only to the particular meaning in the contexts of this book.

CHOG LHUNG TRALWA (*phyogs lhung bral ba*) — without falling into limitations
CHOGZHAG (*cog bzhag*) — remaining as it is, leaving things as they are
CHÖDPA (*spyod pa*) — attitude, behavior
DA (*brda*) — (literally: symbol) the four *das* are a fundamental method of practice in the Longde series of Dzogchen. See LONGDE
DAGMEDMA (*bdag med ma*) — Nairatmya, consort of Hevajra
DANG (*gdangs*) — one of the three ways in which the energy of our primordial state manifests itself
DENGDROL THOGTU CHA (*gdeng grol thog tu 'cha'*) — confidence in liberation gained through continuing in the state of contemplation.
DENNYI SUNJUG (*bden gnyis zung 'jug*) — union of the two truths
DESHEG KAGYED (*bde gshegs bka' brgyad*) — eight Mahayoga *heruka* sadhanas
DEWA (*bde ba*) — pleasurable sensation
DORJE SEMPA (*rdo rje sems dpa'*) — Vajrasattva
DORJE SEMPA NAMKHA CHE (*rdo rje sems dpa' nam mkha' che*) — title of a Dzogchen lung
DORJEI KU (*rdo rje'i sku*) — vajrakaya, dimension of the Vajra
DREBU (*'bras bu*) — fruit
DRIBPA (*sgrib pa*) — obstacle
DZOG (*rdzogs*) — perfected
DZOGPA CHENPO (*rdzogs pa chen po*), Dzogchen (*rdzogs chen*) — the Total Perfection
DZOGRIM (*rdzogs rim*) — completion stage
GAMPOPA (*sgam po pa*) — famous master, a student of Milarepa
GARAB DORJE (*dga' rab rdo rje*) — the first teacher of Dzogchen in our epoch
GELUGPA (*dge lugs pa*) — a Tibetan Buddhist school
GESHE (*dge bshes*) — a learned scholar
GOMPA (*sgom pa*) — meditation

GÖPA (*rgod pa*) — agitation
GYARMA CHEDPA (*rgyar ma chad pa*) — not falling into limitation
GYÜD (*rgyud*) — tantra or root text
GYUWA (*'gyu ba*) — movement
JAMGÖN KONGTRUL RINPOCHE (*'jam mgon kong sprul rin po che*) — a realized master from the Kagyüdpa tradition of Tibetan Buddhism
JAMYANG KHYENTSE WANGPO (*'jam dbyangs mkhyen brtse'i dbang po*) — a realized master from the Sakya tradition of Tibetan Buddhism
JIGMED LINGPA (*'jigs med gling pa*) — a realized master from the Nyingma tradition of Tibetan Buddhism
JIGTEN CHÖTÖD (*'jig rten mchod bstod*) — literally "offering and praise to worldly deities," one of the DESHEG KAGYED
JU MIPHAM (*'ju mi pham*) — a famous master and great scholar from the Nyingma tradition of Tibetan Buddhism
JUGPA (*'jug pa*) — application
KADAG (*ka dag*) — pure from the beginning
KAGYÜDPA (*bka' brgyud pa*) — a Tibetan Buddhist school
KANGZAG (*gang zag*) — person
KHAM (*khams*) — element, realm, dhatu
KHORYUG CHENPO (*khor yug chen po*) — the great horizon
KHUJUG (*khu byug*) — cuckoo
KOMPAI NYAM (*goms pa'i nyams*) — a habitual experience
KUNTUZANG (*kun tu bzang*) — all good, Samantabhadra
KYERIM (*bskyed rim*) — development stage
LABPA (*bslab pa*) — training
LAM (*lam*) — path
LENANG (*las snang*) — karmic vision
LHAGTHONG (*lhag mthong*) — insight
LHÖPA (*lhod pa*) — something that is loosened or relaxed
LHÖPA CHENPO (*lhod pa chen po*) — total relaxation
LHUNDRUB (*lhun grub*) — self-perfected

LHUNGYI (*lhun gyis*) — effortlessly
LHUNGYI NEPA (*lhun gyis gnas pas*) — effortlessly relaxed
LONGDE (*klong sde*) — the Space Series, one of the three series of Dzogchen. Longde is related to the Second Statement of Garab Dorje, "not remaining in doubt"
LONGCHENPA (*klong chen pa*) — a realized master of the Nyingma tradition of Tibetan Buddhism
LUNG (*lung*) — a class of text
MACHIG LABDRÖN (*ma gcig lab sgron*) — a realized woman master who was instrumental in the development of the practice of Chöd
MACHÖPA (*ma bcos pa*) — not corrected
MARIGPA (*ma rig pa*) — ignorance
MINYI (*mi gnyis*) — nondual
MITOG (*mi rtog*) — no thought
MITOGPA (*mi rtog pa*) — without thought, beyond thought
MITÖN (*mi rton*) — not based on
MIYOWA (*mi g.yo ba*) — not moving
MÖNPA (*smon pa*) — intention, aspiration
NAGTSUR (*nag mtshur*) — a mineral used for cleaning gold
NAKHA (*sna kha*) — different types
NALJOR (*rnal 'byor*) — yoga
NAMPA (*rnam pa*) — various
NAMPAR NANGDZED (*rnam par snang mdzad*) — visions are uninterrupted, Vairochana
NAMSHE (*rnam shes*) — consciousness
NANGTONG (*snang stong*) — vision and emptiness
NANGTONG SUNGJUG (*snang stong zung 'jug*) — the union of vision and emptiness
NATSOG (*sna tshogs*) — diversity
NED (*nad*) — illness
NEPA (*gnas pa*) — calm state

NEPAI TINGEDZIN (*gnas pa'i ting nge 'dzin*) — contemplation of the calm state

NEPANG (*nad spang*) — beyond illness

NGEJUNG (*nges 'byung*) — short form of *nges par 'byung ba*; in the context of Sutra it means renunciation, whereas in Dzogchen it means participation

NGO (*ngo*) — one's own condition

NGÖNDRO (*sngon 'gro*) — preliminary practice

NGORANG THOGTU TRED (*ngo rang thog tu 'phrad*) — direct introduction

NGOWO NYIDKU (*ngo bo nyid sku*) — dimension of the union of the three dimensions (literally: bodies)

NYINGMAPA (*rnying ma pa*) — a Tibetan Buddhist school

NYI (*gnyis*) — two

NUBCHEN SANGYE YESHE (*gnubs chen sangs rgyas ye shes*) — a realized master of the Nyingma tradition of Tibetan Buddhism

NYAM (*nyams*) — experience

NYAMNANG (*nyams snang*) — vision of experience

NYID (*nyid*) — the state of itself

NYIMED (*gnyis med*) — nondual

NYINGMA (*rnying ma*) (literally: ancient) — one of the four main schools of Tibetan Buddhism, the other three being Kagyüd, Sakya, and Gelug

PAL (*dpal*) — glory

PALTRUL RINPOCHE (*dpal sprul rin po che*) — a famous nineteenth-century teacher from the Nyingma tradition of Tibetan Buddhism

PANG (*spang*) — abandoned, gone beyond

RANGZHIN (*rang bzhin*) — nature

RIGDZIN (*rig 'dzin*) — knowledge holder, realized being

RIGPA (*rig pa*) — instant presence, state of knowledge

RIGPAI KHUJUG (*rig pa'i khu byug*) — The Cuckoo of Instant Presence

RIMED (*ris med*) — nonsectarian

RIWO CHOGZHAG (*ri bo cog bzhag*) — like a mountain: the first of the four Chogzhags, "remaining as it is."

ROLPA (*rol pa*) — one of the three ways in which the energy of our primordial state manifests itself. See DANG and TSAL.

SA CHIGPA (*sa gcig pa*) — single stage, one single *bhumi*

SAKYAPA (*sa skya pa*) — a Tibetan Buddhist school

SALWA (*gsal ba*) — clarity

SAMATOG (*za ma tog*) — container for keeping objects used in practice

SAMTEN MIGDRÖN (*bsam gtan mig sgron*) — *The Light of the Eye of Contemplation*, title of a text by Nubchen Sangye Yeshe

SEMDE (*sems sde*) — the Primordial Mind Series, one of the three series of Dzogchen. Semde is related to the first statement of Garab Dorje

SEMDZIN (*sems 'dzin*) — a particular type of Dzogchen practice

SEMPA DORJE (*sems dpa' rdo rje*) — Sattvavajra

SHALUNG (*zhwa lung*) — a monastery in Tibet

SHE (*shas*) — something in a group

SHEJAI DRIBPA (*shes bya'i sgrib pa*) — obstacles to knowledge

SHERAB (*shes rab*) — prajña, discriminating wisdom

SHILHAG SUNGJUG (*zhi lhag zung 'jug*) — union of Shine and Lhagthong

SHINE (*zhi gnas*) — calm state

SINPA (*zin pa*) — completed

TAGNANG (*dag snang*) — pure vision

TAMTSIG (*dam tshig*) — samaya, promise

TASHI (*bkra shis*) — good fortune

TASHIPAI PAL RIGPAI KHUJYUG (*bkra shis pa'i dpal rig pa'i khu byug*) — the full title of *The Cuckoo of Presence*

TAWA (*lta ba*) — view

TENPAI NYAM (*brtan pa'i nyams*) — experience of stability

THAB (*thabs*) — method

THAGCHIG (*thag gcig*) — one state, the single presence

THAGCHIG THOGTU CHED (*thag gcig thog tu chad*) — not remaining in doubt
THANGKA (*thang ga* or *thang kha*) — traditional Tibetan painting
THARCHIN (*mthar phyin*) — accomplished
THARCHINPAI NYAM (*mthar phyin pa'i nyams*) — experience of ultimate accomplishment
TINGEDZIN (*ting nge 'dzin*) — contemplation, samadhi
TINGEDZIN KHORYUG CHENPO (*ting nge 'dzin 'khor yug chen po*) — the Great Contemplation
THIGLE CHENPO (*thig le chen po*) — total thigle
THOBPAI NYAM (*thob pa'i nyams*) — experience of attainment
THÖGAL (*thod rgal*) — an advanced practice of Dzogchen related to the aspect of self-perfection of our real nature
TÖN (*don*) — meaning
TÖN (*rton*) — based on, in agreement with
TÖN PA ZHI (*rton pa bzhi*) — the Four Agreements in Meaning
TRANGDON (*drang don*) — conventional meaning
TREGCHÖD (*khregs chod*) — self-loosening of a bundle; the name of a main Dzogchen Upadesha practice
TRISONG DETSEN (*khri srong ldeu btsan*) — ninth-century Tibetan king who invited Padmasambhava and several other Buddhist teachers to Tibet
TRÖTANGTRAL (*spros dang bral*) — beyond judgment, free of conceptual elaborations
TSAL (*rtsal*) — one of the three ways in which the energy of our primordial state manifests itself. See DANG and ROLPA.
TSIG (*tshig*) — word, term
TSOLMED (*rtsol med*) — without effort
TSOLWA (*rtsol ba*) — commitment or effort
TSONGKHAPA (*tsong kha pa*) — the founder of the Gelugpa school of Tibetan Buddhism

WANGPO (*dbang po*) — the senses

WANGPO THOGCHEKYI DÜD (*dbang po thogs bcas kyi bdud*) — one of the four main demons in the practice of Chöd, referring to the clarity of the senses being blocked

YAB-YUM (*yab yum*) — in sexual union

YANGDAGGI TAWA (*yang dag gi lta ba*) — correct point of view

YOWA (*g.yo ba*) — movement, agitation

YOWAI NYAM (*g.yo ba'i nyams*) — experience of movement

YULDEN (*yul bden*) — real object

YULDEN KADAG (*yul bden ka dag*) — primordial purity of appearing objects

YUM (*yum*) — mother, consort

ZHI (*gzhi*) — the base

GLOSSARY
of Sanskrit and Oddiyana Language Terms

ABHIDHARMAKOSHA (*Abhidharmakośa*) — *The Treasury of Abhidharma* by Vasubhandhu, an important text presenting fundamental Buddhist ideas and definitions

ANUTTARATANTRA (*anuttaratantra*) — Highest Yoga Tantra, a class of tantras in Tibetan Buddhism

ANUYOGA (*Anuyoga*) — a class of tantras in the Nyingmapa school of Tibetan Buddhism characterized by instantaneous transformation, as opposed to the gradual transformation applied in Mahayoga

ATI (*Ati*) — a synonym for Dzogchen

ATIYOGA (*Atiyoga*) — a synonym for the Dzogchen teachings

AVALOKITESHVARA (*Avalokiteśvara*) — a realized being also known as the bodhisattva of compassion

BHUMI (*bhūmi*) — various stages of spiritual development of boddhisattvas; there are ten bhumis in Mahayana Buddhism

BODHICHITTA (*bodhicitta*) — in Mahayana: the intention to attain realization for the benefit of all sentient beings and putting this intention into practice; in Dzogchen: the Primordial State of the individual

BODHISATTVA (*bodhisattva*) — a practitioner of Mahayana Buddhism who cultivates the altruistic motivation to achieve enlightenment in order to liberate all sentient beings from suffering

CHAKRA (*cakra*) — an energy center in the body

CHAKRASMVARA (*Cakrasaṃvara*) — a deity belonging to the Anuttaratantra class

DAKINI (*ḍākinī*) — a female embodiment of enlightened energy

DEVA (*deva*) — deity

DHARMAKAYA (*dharmakāya*) — one of the three main dimensions of enlightenment, the absolute dimension

DHATU (*dhātu*) — element, constituent, realm

DOHA (*dohā*) — a song of realization

E VAM (*e vaṃ*) — syllables representing the aspects of emptiness and manifestation, wisdom and method

GANACHAKRA (*Gaṇacakra*) — literally "wheel of gathering," a feast offering

GANAPUJA (*Gaṇapūjā*) — an offering ritual in Tibetan Buddhism; a symbol of Ganachakra

GUHYASAMAJA (*Guhyasamāja*) — a deity belonging to the Anuttaratantra class

GURUYOGA (*Guruyoga*) — a practice of spiritual unification with the state of one's teacher

HERUKA (*he ru ka*) — a wrathful deity

HEVAJRA (*Hevajra*) — a deity belonging to the Anuttaratantra class

HINAYANA (*Hīnayāna*) — one of the two vehicles of the Path of Renunciation, the other one being Mahayana

KALACHAKRA (*Kālacakra*) — a deity belonging to the Anuttaratantra class

KARMA (*karma*) (literally: action) — actions and their positive and negative results; law of cause and effect

KAYA (*kāya*) (literally: body) — a dimension of enlightenment

KRIYATANTRA (*Kriyātantra*) (literally: tantra of action) — a class of tantras in Tibetan Buddhism

KUNDALINI (*kuṇḍalinī*) — a subtle energy related to the physical body

LOKA (*loka*) — a dimension of worldly existence

MAHAMUDRA (*Mahāmudrā*) — the final stage of realization of Anuttaratantra; a meditation tradition in the Kagyüd tradition

MAHASIDDHA (*mahāsiddha*) — a great yogin who achieved extraordinary attainments (*siddhi*)

MAHAYOGA (*Mahāyoga*) — a class of tantras in the Nyingmapa school of Tibetan Buddhism characterized by gradual transformation, as opposed to instantaneous transformation applied in Anuyoga

MALA (*mālā*) — a rosary, usually with 108 beads

MANJUSHRIMITRA (*Mañjuśrīmitra*) — an important scholar and Dzogchen master

MANTRA (*mantra*) — a combination of sounds endowed with spiritual function

MANTRAYANA (*Mantrayāna*) — the Mantra Vehicle, a synonym of Vajrayana

MERU (*Meru*) — mythical mountain in Hindu and Buddhist cosmologies

NAGA (*nāga*) — a class of non-human beings with snake-like form

NAGARJUNA (*Nāgārjuna*) — an important master and scholar of Mahayana Buddhism

NAIRATMYA (*Nairātmyā*) — the consort of Hevajra

NIRMANAKAYA (*nirmāṇakāya*) (literally: the body of manifestation) — different manifestations of enlightened beings visible to sentient beings

PADMASAMBHAVA (*padmasambhava*) — eighth-century Buddhist master responsible for introducing Buddhism to Tibet

PANDIT (*paṇḍita*) — scholar, learned one

PARINIRVANA (*parinirvāṇa*) — passing into nirvana

PRAJNAPARAMITA ABHISAMAYALANKARA (*Prajñāpāramitā Abhisamayālaṅkāra*) — *The Ornament of Clear Realization*, one of the five treatises transmitted by the future Buddha Maitreya to Asanga

PRANA (*prāṇa*) — subtle energy moving through different channels and energy centers (chakras)

PRETA (*preta*) — a hungry ghost, a being that abides in a dimension of permanent suffering caused by hunger and thirst

RATNA (*ratna*) — one of the five Buddha families

RUPAKAYA (*rūpakāya*) — a dimension of enlightenment endowed with form (sambogakaya and nirmanakaya), as opposed to dharmakaya which is a dimension of enlightenment without form

SAMADHI (*samādhi*) — meditative absorption, contemplation

SAMANTABHADRA (*samantabhadra*) — the Primordial Buddha

SAMAYA (*samaya*) — a sacred commitment in Vajrayana

SAMBHOGAKAYA (*saṃbhogakāya*) (literally: the body of enjoyment) — a dimension of enlightenment of pure appearances

SANGHA (*saṃgha*) — a community of practitioners of Buddhism

SARAHA (*Saraha*) — one of the eighty-four famous mahasiddhas

SATTVAVAJRA (*sattvavajra*) — the Vajra of the mind (the nature of the mind)

SHAKYAMUNI (*Śākyamuni*) — the historical Buddha, Siddharta Gautama

SHANTARAKSHITA (*Śāntarakṣita*) — great Mahayana scholar and the abbot of the Nalanda University invited by King Trisong Detsen to establish Buddhism in Tibet

SHUNYATA (*śūnyatā*) — emptiness

SIMHAMUKHA (*Siṃhamukhā*) — lion-faced dakini, a meditational deity with the face similar to that of a snow lion

ŚRI SIMHA (*Śrī Siṃha*) — great Dzogchen master, student of Manjushrimitra and teacher of Jnanasutra, Vimalamitra, Padmasambhava and Vairochana

SUTRA (*sūtra*) — in this context, the Buddhist Path of Renunciation

TANTRA (*tantra*) — in this context, the Buddhist Path of Transformation

TARA (*Tārā*) — a female Buddha associated with compassion and enlightened activity.

TATHAGATA (*tathāgata*) (literally: thus-gone) — an epithet of a buddha

UPADESHA (*Upadeśa*) — one of the three series of Dzogchen related to the third statement of Garab Dorje

UPASAKA (*upāsaka*) — a lay practitioner

VAIROCHANA (*vairocana*) — great Dzogchen master and translator at the time of King Trisong Detsen

VAJRAKAYA (*vajrakāya*) — an unchanging dimension of enlightenment

VIMALAMITRA (*vimalamitra*) — great Dzogchen master invited to Tibet by King Trisong Detsen

VINAYA (*vinaya*) — a collection of Buddha's teachings related to monastic discipline

VIRUPA (*Virūpa*) — one of the eighty-four famous mahasiddhas

YANTRA YOGA (*yantrayoga*) — a system of breathing connected with movements used to master one's prana energy (*rlung*), subtle channels (*rtsa*) and the potentiality of energy (*thig le*)

YOGATANTRA (*Yogatantra*) — a class of tantras in Tibetan Buddhism

www.ingramcontent.com/pod-product-compliance
Lightning Source LLC
Chambersburg PA
CBHW032001080426
42735CB00007B/476